FOUR AMERICAN POETS: WILLIAM CULLEN BRYANT, HENRY WADSWORTH LONGFELLOW, JOHN GREENLEAF WHITTIER, OLIVER WENDELL HOLMES. A BOOK FOR YOUNG AMERICANS

Published @ 2017 Trieste Publishing Pty Ltd

ISBN 9780649587278

Four American Poets: William Cullen Bryant, Henry Wadsworth Longfellow, John Greenleaf Whittier, Oliver Wendell Holmes. A Book for Young Americans by Sherwin Cody

Edited by Trieste Publishing Pty Ltd.
Cover @ 2017

www.triestepublishing.com

SHERWIN CODY

FOUR AMERICAN POETS: WILLIAM CULLEN BRYANT, HENRY WADSWORTH LONGFELLOW, JOHN GREENLEAF WHITTIER, OLIVER WENDELL HOLMES. A BOOK FOR YOUNG AMERICANS

 Trieste

FOUR AMERICAN POETS

William Cullen Bryant
. Henry Wadsworth Longfellow
John Greenleaf Whittier
Oliver Wendell Holmes

· A BOOK FOR YOUNG AMERICANS

BY

SHERWIN _CODY

Author of "The Art of Short Story Writing," "Story Composition,"
"In the Heart of the Hills," etc.

WERNER SCHOOL BOOK COMPANY

NEW YORK   CHICAGO   BOSTON

594378

THE C
FOUR GREAT AMERICANS SERIES
Biographical Stories of Great Americans for Young Americans

EDITED BY
JAMES BALDWIN, Ph.D.

I N these biographical stories the lives of great Americans are presented in such a manner as to hold the attention of the youngest reader. In these lives the child finds the most inspiring examples of good citizenship and true patriotism.

VOLUMES NOW READY:

I. FOUR GREAT AMERICANS
GEORGE WASHINGTON, BENJAMIN FRANKLIN
DANIEL WEBSTER, ABRAHAM LINCOLN
By JAMES BALDWIN, Ph.D.

Cloth, 246 pages, - · · - Price, 50 cents

II. FOUR AMERICAN PATRIOTS
PATRICK HENRY, ALEXANDER HAMILTON
ANDREW JACKSON, U. S. GRANT
By ALMA HOLMAN BURTON
Author of "The Story of Our Country," etc.

Cloth, 254 pages, - · · - Price, 50 cents

III. FOUR AMERICAN NAVAL HEROES
PAUL JONES, OLIVER H. PERRY
ADMIRAL FARRAGUT, ADMIRAL DEWEY
By MABEL BORTON BEEBE

Cloth, 254 pages. - · · - Price, 50 cents

IV. FOUR AMERICAN POETS
WILLIAM CULLEN BRYANT, HENRY WADSWORTH
LONGFELLOW, JOHN GREENLEAF WHITTIER
OLIVER WENDELL HOLMES
By SHERWIN CODY

Cloth, 254 pages, - · - - Price, 50 cents

OTHER VOLUMES IN PRAPARATION

COPYRIGHT, 1899, BY WERNER SCHOOL BOOK COMPANY

The Lakeside Press
R. R. DONNELLEY & SONS COMPANY
CHICAGO

CONTENTS

THE STORY OF WILLIAM CULLEN BRYANT

THE STORY OF HENRY W. LONGFELLOW

3

4   CONTENTS

THE STORY OF JOHN GREENLEAF WHITTIER

THE STORY OF OLIVER WENDELL HOLMES

THE STORY OF

WILLIAM CULLEN BRYANT

WILLIAM CULLEN BRYANT

BRYANT

CHAPTER I

THE LOVE OF NATURE

Do you know what is meant by "the love of Nature"? Yes? But are you quite sure? Think a little. It is not an easy thing to understand, and many older people than you do not know what it means.

Bryant was the great American poet of Nature. His poetry is best understood and enjoyed by those who have first learned to love Nature as he loved her. To all such it appears to be very simple and grand.

In order that we may come by easy steps to a true appreciation of Bryant's poetry, let us take a lesson in the love of Nature.

"Man made the city, God made the country,"

is the old saying. Look at the long rows of city houses : how ugly they are! How dirty are the streets, from which on windy days clouds of dust sometimes rise and almost choke you as you walk along! Even the sky above is not often clear and blue as it ought to be, but it seems filthy with smoke and soot. And what sounds you hear! The noise of the cars as they buzz and jar along the street, the monotonous roar of human traffic, and the rough words of teamsters and hackmen as they try to crowd by one another —all these grate upon the sensitive ear.

How different is everything in the country! What a clear, brilliant blue the sky is; and what a vast variety of color the surface of the earth presents!

Here is the light, fresh green of the grass, and over there are the darker greens of the pines and cedars. In the autumn we observe the gorgeous hues of the maples and the oaks as their leaves change with the frost from green to crimson and gold. Think, too, of the flowers! Here are fields white with daisies,

and there are other fields filled with yellow butter-
cups or red clover blossoms! Farther away are
fields of the graceful, slender-stalked wheat, or of
the tall, rustling corn!

Have you ever been in the woods in June? Instead of the harsh sounds of the streets, you
hear the tumultuous but harmonious songs of
birds; instead of the steady roar of traffic,
you hear the deep note of the wind through
the trees, or the murmur of a little brook flowing
over stones or dashing down a waterfall. All
around you the trees rise, like columns in a cathe-
dral, but more beautiful and majestic; and the air
is filled with a sweet scent fit to be used for
incense in the churches.

Now read what Bryant has to say in his "In-
scription for the Entrance to a Wood." There are
many hard words in it, and you must read very
carefully and thoughtfully; but it will make you
feel that on entering such a wood you are indeed
going into God's own natural church, a place even
more magnificent and wonderful than Solomon's
temple:

Stranger, if thou hast learned a truth which needs
No school of long experience, that the world
Is full of guilt and misery, and hast seen
Enough of all its sorrows, crimes, and cares
To tire thee of it, enter this wild wood
And view the haunts of Nature. The calm shade
Shall bring a kindred calm, and the sweet breeze
That makes the green leaves dance, shall waft a balm
To thy sick heart. Thou wilt find nothing here
Of all that pained thee in the haunts of men,
And made thee loathe thy life. The primal curse
Fell, it is true, upon the unsinning earth,
But not in vengeance. God hath yoked to guilt
Her pale tormentor, misery. Hence these shades
Are still the abodes of gladness; the thick roof
Of green and stirring branches is alive
And musical with birds, that sing and sport
In wantonness of spirit; while below
The squirrel, with raised paws and form erect,
Chirps merrily. Throngs of insects in the shade
Try their thin wings and dance in the warm beam
That waked them into life. Even the green trees
Partake the deep contentment; as they bend
To the soft winds, the sun from the blue sky
Looks in and sheds a blessing on the scene.
Scarce less the cleft-born wild-flower seems to enjoy

Existence, than the wingèd plunderer
That sucks its sweets. The mossy rocks themselves,
And the old and ponderous trunks of prostrate trees
That lead from knoll to knoll a causey rude
Or bridge the sunken brook, and their dark roots,
With all their earth upon them, twisting high,
Breathe fixed tranquillity. The rivulet
Sends forth glad sounds, and tripping o'er its bed
Of pebbly sands, or leaping down the rocks,
Seems, with continuous laughter, to rejoice
In its own being. Softly tread the marge,
Lest from her midway perch thou scare the wren
That dips her bill in water. The cool wind
That stirs the stream in play, shall come to thee,
Like one that loves thee, nor let thee pass
Ungreeted, and shall give its light embrace.*

This is one of the hardest things in Bryant's
poetry. When you can see all its beauties, and
take pleasure in reading it, you will have learned
to love both Nature and Nature's poet-priest.

* To help in the mastery of this poem, the student is advised to make
a careful list of all the natural objects mentioned in it, such as birds,
brooks, trees, and flowers, and try to recollect having seen something
of the same sort.

CHAPTER II

BRYANT'S CHILDHOOD

Bryant was the first great American poet, having been born fourteen years before Longfellow. Like Longfellow, he could trace his descent (on his mother's side) from John Alden and Priscilla Mullens, who came over in the *Mayflower;* and through two other branches he was descended from Pilgrim stock. The first Bryant in America did not come in the *Mayflower*, but he was in Plymouth in 1632, and was chosen town constable in 1663.

The poet's father and grandfather were both doctors; so when Dr. Peter Bryant was married to "sweet Sallie Snell," as the poet has it, and their second child was born, the good doctor named him William Cullen, after a great medical authority who had died four years before. This happy event—that is, the birth of William Cullen Bryant —occurred November 3, 1794, in the small town of Cummington, Massachusetts. But instead of growing up to be a doctor the boy became a poet, and his father was rather proud of the fact, too.

Cummington is a small town among the Berkshire hills, in the western part of Massachusetts. The country around it is mountainous, with wide valleys which in the early days were very fertile. Bryant's grandfather, Snell, had come here in 1774, just before the Revolution, with a handful of other settlers, to take up a homestead. There is a story that Eben Snell, Jr., an uncle of the poet, while working in the cornfield put his ear to the ground and heard the sounds of the distant battle of Bunker Hill.

Little William Cullen was very quick and bright, though puny. In his autobiography he says he could go alone when he was but a year old, and knew all the letters of the alphabet four months later. His older brother, Austin, did even better than this, however; for he began to read the Bible before he was three years old, and in just about a year from the time he began, he had read it all through, from Genesis to Revelation. William Cullen as a small child learned many of Watts's hymns, and used to recite them as he stood by his mother's knee.

It is probable that so much study was not good for him, for he suffered from terrible headaches, and was so puny his father and mother thought he would not live long. His head seemed to be too big for his body. There is a story that some medical students, who were studying in Dr. Bryant's office when William was a child, were ordered to give him a cold bath every morning in a spring near the house. They kept this up so late in the fall that they had to break the first skim of ice on the top of the water. The treatment cured him, and after he was fourteen, he says, he never had a headache in his life.

He began to go to school before he was four years old. It was not unnatural that a little fellow of that age should get sleepy during school hours. One day he woke from a sound nap to find himself in his teacher's lap. When he realized where he was he became furiously angry at the thought that he should be treated so like a baby.

About this time, too, he was kicked by a horse. A lady had come to call on his mother, and had tied her horse to a tree near the door. There were fresh chips scattered about, and William and his elder brother amused themselves by throwing them at the horse's heels to make him caper. William got too near and at last the horse kicked him over. He soon recovered, and went to school with a bandaged head, but a scar from the wound on his head he carried to the day of his death.

When he was five years old, the family went to live on Grandfather Snell's old homestead, where Dr. Peter Bryant remained as long as he lived. Years afterward, when the poet became rich, he bought this place for a country home.

He began now to go regularly to the district school, where he learned reading, writing, and arithmetic, a little grammar and geography, and the Westminster Catechism. He was a fine speller, seldom missing a word, and he got on well in geography. The catechism, however, did not interest him and he could not understand it.

Those were very strict Puritanic days. Says Bryant, in his autobiography: "One of the means of keeping boys in order was a little bundle of birchen rods, bound together with a small cord, and generally suspended on a nail against the kitchen wall. This was esteemed as much a part of the necessary furniture as the crane that hung in the kitchen fireplace, or the shovel and tongs." And he tells us that sometimes the boy was sent out to cut the twigs with which he himself was to be whipped.

Not only was whipping thought to be good for boys, but even grown-up people were whipped in public for petty crimes.

About a mile from the Bryant home was a public whipping-post. Says the poet: "I remember seeing a young fellow, of about eighteen years of age, upon whose back, by direction of a justice of the peace, forty lashes had just been laid, as the punishment for a theft which he had committed. His eyes were red, like those of one who had been crying, and I well remember the feeling of curiosity, mingled with pity and fear, with which I gazed on him."

This was the last time the whipping-post was used in that neighborhood, but it stood there for several years longer.

CHAPTER III

WHAT THE BOYS DID WHEN BRYANT WAS YOUNG

Life in the time of Bryant's boyhood was rather
hard and rough. New England country life was
never easy. The chairs were very straight-backed,
the beds were hard, and the food was not very
delicate, though there was always plenty of it—
plenty of pork and beans, if nothing else. For all
that, the boys in Bryant's day had a very good
time, which he tells about in the account of his
early life to which we have already referred.

Among the pleasant occurrences of those old-
fashioned times were the neighborhood "raisings."
When a man intended to build a house he got
all the big, heavy timbers together for the frame,
and then called in the neighbors to help him put
them up. The minister always made a point of
being present; and the young men thought it great
sport, as did the boys, who could only look on. "It
was a spectacle for us," says Bryant, "next to that
of a performer on the tight-rope, to see the young
men walk steadily on the narrow footing of the

beams at a great height from the ground, or as
they stood to catch in their hands the wooden pins
and the braces flung to them from below. Each
tried to outdo the other in daring, and when the
frame was all up, one of them would usually cap the
climax by standing on his head on the ridge-pole."

Another good time was had at the maple sugar
frolic. In spring, when the sap begins to come
up in the maple trees, men go about, and bore two
or three holes in every maple tree in a sugar
camp. In these they stick little spigots with holes
through them, and underneath they set a pail to
catch the sap. Soon it begins to drop. When the
pails are filled, the men bring fresh ones, and carry
off the sap to an enormous iron kettle hung on a
pole over a hot fire.

"From my father's door," says Bryant, "in the
latter part of March and the early part of April,
we could see a dozen columns of smoke rising over
the woods in different places, where the work was
going on. After the sap had been collected and
boiled for three or four days, the time came when
the thickening liquid was made to pass into the

form of sugar. This was when the syrup had become of such a consistency that it would feather—that is to say, when a beechen twig, formed at the small end into a little loop, dipped into the hot syrup and blown upon by the breath, sent into the air a light, feathery film." The syrup was then lifted off and poured into moulds, or else stirred rapidly until cooled, when it became delicious brown sugar in loose grains. The boys had a great deal of fun "trying" the syrup to see if it was ready to "sugar off."

Then there were husking-bees and apple-parings and cider-making ; and in the winter all the young people went to singing school.

Bryant in his boyhood was also fond of fishing for trout in the small streams, where there were plenty of fish to catch. Another sport was squirrel shooting. The young men would divide into two equal parties and see which party could shoot the most squirrels.

Of course, in those days everybody went to church. Young Bryant began when he was only three years old. History does not say how he

behaved, but there was not much chance to be
naughty in church in those times. Every parish
had its tithing man, whose business it was to
maintain order in the church during divine serv-
ice, and who sat with a stern countenance through
the sermon, keeping a vigilant eye on the boys in
distant pews and in the galleries. Sometimes
when he detected two of them communicating
with each other, he went to one of them, took him
by the arm, and leading him away, seated him
beside himself. He was also directed by law to see
that the Sabbath was not profaned by people
wandering in the fields or fishing in the brooks.

When he was eight years old, young Cullen
began to make poetry. His grandfather thought
him rather bright at this, and a year or two later
asked him to turn the first chapter of the Book
of Job into verse. He did it all. Here are two
sample lines :

His name was Job, evil he did eschew.
To him were born seven sons; three daughters, too.

For this he received a ninepenny piece, though
his father thought the lines rather bad.

CHAPTER IV

THE YOUNG POET

Bryant's poetic career began when he was twelve years old. Besides some "Enigmas" and a translation from the Latin of Horace, he made a copy of verses to be recited at the close of the winter school, "in the presence of the master, the minister of the parish, and a number of private gentlemen." The verses were printed in the *Hampshire Gazette*, March 18, 1806, the year before Longfellow was born. This same newspaper had other contributions also from the pen of "C. B."

Dr. Peter Bryant was something of a politician. He was several times a representative in the Massachusetts legislature, and finally a senator. He belonged to the Federal party, which corresponds to the present Republican party. Jefferson was president, and in 1807 he laid an embargo on shipping. This stopped all commerce and brought on severe hard times, at which all the members of the party opposed to Jefferson were very indignant.

Dr. Bryant thought his young son might write a satirical poem about it. So "The Embargo; or, Sketches of the Times," was written and printed in a volume. There was a line on the title page saying the poem was written by "a youth of thirteen." One of the great periodicals of that time, called the *Anthology*, reviewed the book, and while speaking well of it, said it seemed impossible that such a poem had been written by a "youth of thirteen." So when the first edition was sold and a second was printed the following year, young Bryant's friends prefixed an "Advertisement," as they called it—a paragraph in which they assured the public that the author was only thirteen, and there were plenty of people who would vouch for it. In this edition the name William Cullen Bryant was boldly printed.

Of course this was not very good poetry. There is a story that years afterward some one asked Bryant if he had a copy of his first book, "The Embargo." "No," said he. Afterward the friend who had asked him said he had found a copy in Boston. "I don't see how you can spend your time with such rubbish," said the poet, and turned away.

During the next few years he wrote other boyish and patriotic poems, some of which were printed in the *Hampshire Gazette*. One, written when he was sixteen, was entitled "The Genius of Columbia"; another was, "An Ode for the Fourth of July, 1812."

In 1812 he entered the Sophomore Class in Williams College, where he remained only a year. There were only the president, one professor, and two tutors at Williams College in those days, and so Bryant's room-mate decided to go to Yale, where he could get a better education. Bryant thought he would go, too. He left Williams College and went home to prepare himself to pass the examinations for entrance to the Junior Class in Yale.

During this summer, while he was studying at home, he often wandered about in the woods; and here he wrote "Thanatopsis." At this time Bryant was a very meditative young man, fond of reading poetry, a fair Greek and Latin scholar, and devotedly fond of the country and all its beauties.

Just how or when he wrote "Thanatopsis" nobody ever knew. In the autumn his father decided that he could not afford to send him to Yale, as he was poor and had a large family. So the young man went away to study law. After he was gone, Dr. Bryant was looking over some papers in his desk, and found in one of the pigeon-holes some poems which his son Cullen had written. One of them was "Thanatopsis." He read it over, and thought it so good that he took it to a lady friend of his.

"Here are some poems," said he, "which our Cullen has been writing."

She took them and began to read. When she had finished "Thanatopsis" she burst into tears; and Dr. Bryant found his eyes rather watery, too.

At that time Dr. Bryant was a member of the senate in the Massachusetts legislature; and so, going up to Boston, he took this and some other poems along. The *North American Review* was the great magazine in those days, and Dr. Bryant knew slightly one of the editors, whose name was Phillips. He went to call on him, but not finding him at home left the package of manuscript with his own name on it. When Mr Phillips came home he found it, and after reading the poems concluded that Dr. Bryant must have written "Thanatopsis," while the other poems were by his son Cullen. But he regarded this poem as such a find that he hurried over to Cambridge to see his two fellow-editors and read them the wonderful lines. When he had finished, one of them, Richard H. Dana, himself a poet, said :

"Oh, Phillips, you have been imposed on. There is no one in America who can write such a poem as that."

"Ah, but I know the man who wrote it," said Phillips. "He is in the senate."

"Well, I must have a look at the man who wrote that poem," said Dana; and off he posted to Boston. He went to the state house, and to the senate chamber, and asked for Senator Bryant. A tall, gray-bearded old man was pointed out to him. Dana looked at him for a few minutes and said to himself: "He has a fine head ; but that man never wrote ' Thanatopsis.'" So without speaking to him he returned to Cambridge.

The poem was printed in the *North American Review.* It was the first great poem ever produced in America ; it was the work of a young man not eighteen years of age, and it has since been said to be the greatest poem ever written by one so young.

CHAPTER V

THANATOPSIS

Every child at school becomes familiar with this grand poem, because it is in many of the higher readers. But that is not enough. You should learn to understand its meaning. As you read this poem, are you not reminded of the deep notes of a church organ, as the organist, left alone, plays some mighty fugue in preparation for the funeral of a great man? Thanatopsis (made up from two Greek words) means a view of death. The poem opens by calling to our minds the grandeurs and the beauty of a cathedral-like wood, where Nature rules supreme.

> To him who in the love of Nature holds
> Communion with her visible forms, she speaks
> A various language; for his gayer hours she
> Has a voice of gladness, and a smile
> And eloquence of beauty, and she glides
> Into his darker musings with a mild
> And healing sympathy, that steals away
> Their sharpness ere he is aware.

We should hardly expect a young man of seventeen to be meditating on death; but even very young people often think about it.

> When thoughts
> Of the last bitter hour come like a blight
> Over thy spirit, and sad images
> Of the stern agony, and shroud, and pall,
> And breathless darkness, and the narrow house,
> Make thee to shudder and grow sick at heart—

These are the things we all think of when father or mother or brother or sister or young friend dies and is laid away in the earth. It is sad and terrible, and we cannot help weeping. At those times

strong men and women shed tears, and we do not
think it strange.   But, says Bryant,—

Go forth under the open sky and list
To Nature's teachings, while from all around—
Earth and her waters, and the depths of air—
Comes a still voice: Yet a few days, and thee
The all-beholding sun shall see no more
In all his course; nor yet in the cold ground,
Where thy pale form was laid, with many tears,
Nor in the embrace of ocean, shall exist
Thy image.   Earth, that nourished thee, shall claim
Thy growth, to be resolved to earth again;
And, lost each human trace, surrendering up
Thine individual being, shalt thou go
To mix forever with the elements,
To be a brother to the insensible rock
And to the sluggish clod, which the rude swain
Turns with his share, and treads upon.   The oak
Shall send his roots abroad and pierce thy mould.
    Yet not to thine eternal resting-place
Shalt thou retire alone, nor couldst thou wish
Couch more magnificent.   Thou shalt lie down
With patriarchs of the infant world—with kings,
The powerful of the earth—the wise, the good,
Fair forms, and hoary seers of ages past,
All in one mighty sepulchre.

Being turned back to earth again does not seem
so terrible when we think that all must have the
same fate. There is a suggestion of grandeur
in the thought that George Washington, King
Solomon, Sir Isaac Newton, Napoleon—all lie in .
the same bed which Nature, the all-ruling, ever-
lasting power, has provided.

> The hills,
> Rock-ribbed and ancient as the sun,—the vales,
> Stretching in pensive quietness between;
> The venerable woods,—rivers that move
> In majesty, and the complaining brooks
> That make the meadows green; and, poured round all,
> Old Ocean's gray and melancholy waste,—
> Are but the solemn decorations all
> Of the great tomb of man.

When we reflect on how many have lived and
died, the earth seems but one great tomb. There
are said to be over 1,200,000,000 persons on the
earth to-day. In a few years they will all have
passed away, and others will have taken their
places; and this change has been going on for thousands and thousands of years. In the graveyards

of any city will be found but a few hundred or at most a few thousand graves; yet hundreds of thousands of people have died there and been buried. Where are their graves?   Lost and forgotten.

                       All that tread
The globe are but a handful to the tribes
That slumber in its bosom.—Take the wings
Of morning, pierce the Barcan wilderness,
Or lose thyself in the continuous woods
Where rolls the Oregon, and hears no sound
Save his own dashings—yet the dead are there:
And millions in those solitudes, since first
The flight of years began, have laid them down
In their last sleep—the dead reign there alone.
So shalt thou rest; and what if thou withdraw
In silence from the living, and no friend
Take note of thy departure?   All that breathe
Will share thy destiny.   The gay will laugh
When thou art gone, the solemn brood of care
Plod on, and each one as before will chase
His favorite phantom; yet all these shall leave
Their mirth and their employments, and shall come
And make their bed with thee.   As the long train
Of ages glides away, the sons of men,
The youth in life's green spring, and he who goes
In the full strength of years, matron and maid,

The speechless babe, and the grey-headed man—
Shall one by one be gathered to thy side,
By those who in their turn shall follow them.

So live that when thy summons comes to join
The innumerable caravan, which moves
To that mysterious realm where each shall take
His chamber in the silent halls of death,
Thou go not, like the quarry-slave at night,
Scourged to his dungeon, but sustained and soothed
By an unfaltering trust, approach thy grave
Like one who wraps the drapery of his couch
About him, and lies down to pleasant dreams.

CHAPTER VI

BRYANT BECOMES A LAWYER

Always of a studious turn, always reading in his father's well-stocked library, or wandering through the woods and writing poetry, Bryant naturally tended towards some learned profession. He did not care to be a doctor; he would have liked to be a literary man, if such a career had then existed or been dreamed possible. As it was not, he finally decided to become a lawyer.

A classmate who remembers him at this time describes him as singularly handsome and finely formed. He was tall and slender, and had a prolific growth of dark brown hair. He was also quick and dextrous in his movements, so much so that his younger brother sometimes boasted about his "stout brother," though he afterward learned that his strength was not so remarkable as his skill and alertness in the use of it.

When his father's poverty compelled him to abandon college, he entered the law office of a Mr. Howe, of Worthington, a quiet little village four or five miles from Cummington.

Bryant's friend and biographer, John Bigelow, says: "A young man's first year's study of the law commonly affects him like his first cigar or his first experience 'before the mast.'" In other words, Bryant didn't like it at all. He was a conscientious young man, and kept at the work; but he felt that he would almost as soon go out as a day laborer. In a letter he speaks of Worthington as consisting of "a blacksmith shop and a cow stable," where his only entertainment was reading

Irving's "Knickerbocker." Mr. Howe complained that he gave more time to Wordsworth's lyrical ballads than to Blackstone and Chitty, the great authorities on law, which he should have been studying.

Young Bryant wanted to go to Boston to continue his studies; but finally, as his father was too poor to support him in Boston, he went to Bridgewater, where his grandfather, Dr. Philip Bryant, lived. He liked this place better. He was poet for a Fourth of July celebration, and became interested in politics. The War of 1812 was going on. Madison was President, and Bryant, in his letters to his friends, speaks of him as "His Imbecility." "His Imbecility" was warned that if he imposed any more taxes the people would revolt.

At one time, Bryant thought of entering the militia for the defense of states' rights. It seems that he then advocated the policy of Massachusetts seceding from the Union, as the Southern states afterwards did.

His father actually got him a commission as adjutant in the Massachusetts militia, but the war

ended, and Bryant kept on with his law studies.
That same year he came of age and was admitted
to practice at the bar.

He now went home and began to look about
for a place where he could begin the practice of law.
He decided on Plainfield, a small village four
or five miles from Cummington. Plainfield had
been the home of his father for a short time when
the future poet was a child ; but it was a very
small place, with not more than two hundred inhab-
itants.

He drudged here for a few months, earning
quite a little money ; but he decided that the
place was too small, and went to Great Barrington, where he had a chance to go into partnership
with a lawyer already established, whose practice
was worth $1,200 a year.

Here he settled down to hard work, and here
he remained as long as he continued to practice
law. After the success of "Thanatopsis," he contributed various articles to the *North American
Review*, and in it were published some of his most
famous poems. He was chosen one of the tithing

men of the town, and soon afterwards town clerk, an office he held for five years. As town clerk he received a salary of five dollars a year. The governor of Massachusetts also made him Justice of the Peace.

When Bryant was twenty-five years old his father died. This caused him great grief ; but about this time, great happiness came to him also. Soon after going to Great Barrington he had become acquainted with a Miss Fairchild, who was an orphan visiting in the neighborhood. He liked her, and the year after his father's death they were married. She was his devoted wife and friend for forty-five years, until she died.

CHAPTER VII

A LITERARY ADVENTURER

Gradually Bryant had become known in the small literary circle that had sprung up around the *North American Review*, though his name was not known outside this small circle in Boston. He had a great desire to become a literary man ; but he knew he must support his wife and family, and verse-making offered no money return.

His friends, Richard H. Dana, Miss Cathe-rine Sedgwick, and one or two others, tried to persuade him to go to New York and engage in literature. Finally he made a visit to New York. A publishing firm there offered him two hundred dollars a year to write one hundred lines of poetry a month for them. He thought this might keep him from starvation. He went back to Great Barrington and stayed for some time longer, con-tributing to the *United States Literary Gazette*, for which Longfellow was then writing.

In 1825 he visited New York again, and was offered the editorship of a monthly periodical, the *New York Review and Athenæum Magazine*, which some publishers were proposing to start. His sal-ary was to be one thousand dollars a year. This offer he accepted, and he went to New York to live, leaving his wife and family in Great Barring-ton until he should find out whether he was going to succeed. He considered that if literature failed, he could drudge at the law in New York as well as at Great Barrington.

James Fenimore Cooper, who was now becoming a famous novelist, was a friend of Bryant's. So was William Ware, who wrote a novel based on the life of Zenobia, the queen of Palmyra,—a very famous book in its day and one still worth reading. Bryant worked very hard. He liked literature a great deal better than he did the law ; and though it was uncertain, he thought that fortune would favor him in the end. The magazine he edited did not succeed very well, and at the end of a year was united with another one, the *New York Literary Gazette.* A few months later the *United States Gazette* in Boston was united with the magazine which Bryant was editing, under the title, *United States Review and Literary Gazette.*

Bryant was allowed one quarter interest in the business and five hundred dollars a year salary. The five hundred dollars was probably all he got, and this sum was so small he could not make it support his family very well. If this magazine should succeed, he would get more money; but it did not, and **Bryant** really thought he would have to quit literature for law once more.

He was licensed to practice in New York; but just then fortune favored him : he was asked to to do some work on the New York *Evening Post.* The assistant editor had gone to Cuba, and finally died there. So Bryant was soon made the assistant editor, and was allowed an interest in the paper.

At that time the paper was favorable to the federal party; but a few years later it became decidedly democratic in tone. So long as Mr. Bryant controlled it, it was an advocate of free trade and a bold champion of human liberty.

CHAPTER VIII

THE EDITOR OF A GREAT NEWSPAPER

Bryant's life work proved to be, not writing poetry, but editing a great New York daily paper. For many years he went to his office at seven o'clock every morning. He was never strong in body, and he had to take very great care of his health.

Every young reader should learn a useful lesson from him, although it is not easy to follow the rigorous mode of life he laid out for himself and followed to the end of his days. He himself tells in a letter what he did :

"I rise early at this time of the year (March), about half-past five ; in summer, half an hour or even an hour earlier. Immediately, with very little encumbrance of clothing, I begin a series of exercises, for the most part designed to expand the chest, and at the same time call into action all the muscles and articulations of the body. These are performed with dumb-bells,—the very lightest, covered with flannel,—with a pole, a horizontal bar, and a light chair swung around my head. After a full hour and sometimes more passed in this manner, I bathe from head to foot. When at my place in the country, I sometimes shorten my exercise in the chamber, and, going out, occupy myself in some work which requires brisk motion. After my bath, if breakfast be not ready, I sit down to my studies till I am called. My breakfast is a simple one—hominy and milk, or, in place of hominy, brown bread, or oatmeal, or wheaten grits, and, in season, baked sweet apples. Buckwheat cakes I do not decline, nor any other article of vegetable food, but animal food I never take at breakfast. Tea and coffee I never touch at any time ; sometimes I take a cup of chocolate, which has no narcotic effect, and agrees with me very well. At breakfast I often take fruit, either in its natural state or freshly stewed.

"After breakfast I occupy myself for a while with my studies, and, when in town, I walk down to the office of the *Evening Post*, nearly three miles distant, and after about three hours return, always walking. * * * In town, where I dine late, I take but two meals a day. Fruit makes a considerable part of my diet. My drink is water.

"That I may rise early, I, of course, go to bed early ; in town as early as ten; in the country somewhat earlier. * * * I abominate drugs and narcotics, and have always carefully avoided anything which spurs nature to exertions which it would not otherwise make. Even with my food I do not take the usual condiments, such as pepper and the like."

A man who was so conscientious about eating and drinking and going to bed and getting up in the morning, was the kind of man who would be conscientious in editing a newspaper. In Bryant's early newspaper life a great daily paper was not so much a machine to gather news from every quarter of the globe and serve it up in a sensational style, as a medium for discussing public questions. Nowadays, people often do not even look at the editorial column; but in those days there was so little news they were obliged to read this. It was about the only fresh thing in the paper. Once a week, perhaps, a sailing vessel from Europe would come in with a bundle of European newspapers, from which the editor would clip and reprint a summary of foreign news. It took several days to get news from Washington to New York. Local items were generally sent in by friends of the editor. For years Bryant had but one assistant, and they two did all the reporting, editing, and editorial writing.

Reviews of books were sometimes done outside, and the shipping and financial news was furnished by a sort of City Press Association. It was Bryant's work to write a brilliant editorial or two every morning. Many of these were on politics, others on questions of local public interest. But Bryant tried always to be on the side of right and justice. For years the *Post* was regarded as the leading paper of the people, standing for the rights of the people. Many a time it fought the battles of the great public, and sometimes it won.

A daily paper lasts but for a day; then it is dead and another takes its place. To know how completely a daily paper dies when its day's work is done, so to speak, suppose you try to buy a copy three months old, or a year old. You remember three months ago there were hundreds of thousands of copies printed and distributed. You suppose that you can get a copy at the office of the paper, at any rate. But no; all more than three months old have been destroyed.

In New York there was once a little old shop, kept by a queer old mulatto, known as "Back

Number Bud," who charged a dollar and a half for a one cent paper, less than a year old. This shop of "Back Number Bud's" was, a few years ago, the only place in New York City where back numbers of newspapers could be purchased at any price; and in smaller cities no copies whatever could be obtained, except by chance.

A daily newspaper influences the people to-day, and then dies, and another paper takes its place. But if one man is making that paper every day for fifty years, at the end of fifty years, doing a little every day, he may have succeeded several times in completely revolutionizing public opinion.

Besides Bryant, there were other great newspaper editors in New York. One was Horace Greeley, whose name every child has heard. There were others, too. But none were so faithful as Bryant. For years his newspaper work took so much of his time that he wrote scarcely any poetry at all. But as those numbers of the *Evening Post* are dead and forgotten, we shall never know how much good he did during those years and years of faithful leadership.

CHAPTER IX

HOW BRYANT BECAME RICH

We have already seen that Bryant was born a poor country boy ; that his father was so poor he could not send his son to college more than a year; and that Bryant himself, when he first went to New York, worked for a time at a salary of only five hundred dollars a year.

When he became assistant editor of the *Evening Post*, the editor-in-chief, William Coleman, who was also the chief proprietor, thought it would be well to give a small interest in the paper to one or two young men, so that when the older proprietors died others would be coming on to take their places. An eighth part was given to Bryant, who was to pay for it gradually from the money he could save. Another portion was offered to a friend of his, who decided not to take it.

Three or four years later, when Mr. Coleman died, Bryant was made editor-in-chief, and bought a larger interest in the paper. He finally secured one half. The other half was owned for a time by

a Mr. Burnham, a practical printer. Later, one
of Bryant's assistants, whose name was Leggett,
owned a part interest.

In those days newspapers were not such costly
properties as they are to-day. Bryant always
made a good living, but he regarded the work in
which he was engaged as drudgery.

After he had been in the newspaper work for
some years, he wrote to his brother, who was a
pioneer in Illinois, saying he thought of retiring
from the *Post*, and asking what could be done in
the West with four or five thousand dollars. His
interest at this time was two fifths, so that he
must have valued the paper at about twelve thousand dollars.

About this time, while he was away from
New York, his partner and assistant editor, Mr.
Leggett, nearly ruined the paper. When Bryant
returned he found that it was earning no money,
and that he could not sell his interest at any price.

He therefore set to work to win popularity for
the paper once more. This he succeeded gradually in doing, and during the next ten years there

was an average yearly profit of over $10,000, of which Bryant received a little less than half. In 1850 the yearly profit was $16,000, and in 1860 it was $70,000. If Bryant received $30,000 for his share of the profits of a year's business, he might be regarded as a rich man. After his death, the *Evening Post* was sold for $900,000, of which Bryant's share was half.

During his later years he bought a great deal of land and many houses on Long Island, where he had a country home. He had another country home at Cummington, his grandfather's homestead, where he built a beautiful house. He also traveled a great deal, going to Europe many times, and to other parts of the world.

Thus, by faithful, plodding work for many years Bryant, though a poet, became rich. He was delicate and sympathetic, like all true poets, but he did not indulge in what some have supposed to be the poet's liberty to be reckless and careless. He worked faithfully and very diligently all his life; and in his old age he was well rewarded for all his labor.

CHAPTER X

BRYANT AS AN ORATOR AND PROSE WRITER

When Bryant went to New York it was a comparatively small city. As years passed, it grew in size and wealth, and its newspapers became more important. We have seen how Bryant became rich by his ownership of the *Evening Post.* He also gained in honors. He was the editor of a great daily paper, and he was also a noted poet. His poems had been published both in this country and in London, and many thousands of copies were sold. Bryant was often asked to write poems for great celebrations, or in honor of well-known people. This he always refused to do. But he often made public addresses. When James Fenimore Cooper died, he acted, as it were, as the spokesman of the nation's grief. He pronounced the funeral eulogy upon Irving, and upon many noted people. He was not a great orator like Daniel Webster; but such speeches as these upon the lives of great men have seldom been surpassed.

We must remember, too, that all his life Bryant,

in his editorials, was writing prose. From these editorials it would be easy to select some of the finest pieces of prose writing in our language. As most of them were on the passing events of the day, they have never been reprinted,—they have died with the newspaper. But here is a passage on the emancipation of the slaves which has the ring of true eloquence.

President Lincoln had proposed gradual emancipation.

"Gradual emancipation!" exclaims Bryant. "Have we not suffered enough from slavery without keeping it any longer? Has not blood enough been shed? My friends, if a child of yours were to fall into the fire, would you pull him out gradually? If he were to swallow a dose of laudanum sufficient to cause speedy death, and a stomach pump were at hand, would you draw out the poison by degrees? If your house were on fire, would you put it out piecemeal? And yet there are men who talk of gradual emancipation by force of ancient habit, and there are men in the slave states who make of slavery a sort of idol which they are unwilling to part with; which, if it must be removed, they would prefer to see removed after a lapse of time and tender leave-takings.

"Slavery is a foul and monstrous idol, a Juggernaut under which thousands are crushed to death; it is a Moloch for whom the children of the land pass through fire. Must we consent that the number of the victims shall be diminished gradually? If there are a thousand·victims this year, are you willing that nine hundred shall be sacrificed next year, and eight hundred the next, and so on until after the lapse of ten years it shall cease? No, my friends, let us hurl the grim image from its pedestal. Down with it to the ground! Dash it to fragments; trample it in the dust. Grind it to powder as the prophets of old commanded that the graven images of the Hebrew idolaters should be ground, and in that state scatter it to the four winds and strew it upon the waters, that no human hand shall ever gather up the accursed atoms and mould them into an image to be worshiped again with human sacrifice."

This eloquent passage is taken from an editorial

in the *Evening Post.* The following is from a
speech delivered at a dinner given to Professor
Morse, the inventor of the telegraph:

"There is one view of this great invention which
impresses me with awe. Beside me at this board,
along with the illustrious man whom we are met to
honor, and whose name will go down to the latest
generations of civilized man, sits the gentleman to
whose clear-sighted perseverance, and to whose
energy—an energy which knew no discouragement,
no weariness, no pause—we owe it that the telegraph has been laid which connects the Old World
with the New through the Atlantic Ocean. My
imagination goes down to the chambers of the
middle sea, to those vast depths where repose the
mystic wire on beds of coral, among forests of
tangle, or on the bottom of the dim blue gulfs,
strewn with the bones of whales and sharks,
skeletons of drowned men, and ribs and masts of
foundered barks, laden with wedges of gold never
to be coined, and pipes of the choicest vintages of
earth never to be tasted.

"Through these watery solitudes, among the

fountains of the great deep, the abode of perpetual silence, never visited by living human presence and beyond the sight of human eye, there are gliding to and fro, by night and by day, in light and in darkness, in calm and in tempest, currents of human thought borne by the electric pulse which obeys the bidding of man. That slender wire thrills with the hopes and fears of nations; it vibrates to every emotion that can be awakened by any event affecting the welfare of the human race.

"A volume of contemporary history passes every hour of the day from one continent to another. An operator on the continent of Europe gently touches the keys of an instrument in his quiet room, a message is shot with the swiftness of light through the abysses of the sea, and before his hand is lifted from the machine the story of revolts and revolutions, of monarchs dethroned and new dynasties set up in their place, of battles and conquests and treaties of peace, of great statesmen fallen in death, lights of the world gone out and new luminaries glimmering on the horizon, is written down in another quiet room on the other side of the globe.

"Mr. President, I see in the circumstances which I have enumerated a new proof of the superiority of mind to matter, of the independent existence of that part of our nature which we call the spirit, when it can thus subdue, enslave, and educate the subtilest, the most active, and in certain of its manifestations the most intractable and terrible, of the elements, making it in our hands the vehicle of thought, and compelling it to speak every language of the civilized world. I infer the capacity of the spirit for a separate state of being, its indestructible essence and its noble destiny, and I thank the great discoverer whom we have assembled to honor for this confirmation of my faith."

CHAPTER XI

OTHER EVENTS IN BRYANT'S LIFE

Among the remaining important events of the poet's life, we must first speak of the publication of his poems. In 1822, the year after his marriage and while he was trying to practice law at Great Barrington, he was invited to deliver the usual poetical address before the Phi Beta Kappa Society of Harvard College. For this occasion he wrote the poem of "The Ages," with which his collected works now open. This poem secured him so much reputation that he published a very small volume of his works. There were but forty-four pages, but in that small space were printed some of the finest poems Bryant ever wrote. The copies did not sell very rapidly, and Bryant's profit was not large. When he was old and famous, a young man said to him, "I have just bought a copy of the first volume of your poems. I paid twenty dollars for it."

"Hm!" said Bryant. "A good deal more than I got for writing it!"

Of his other poems, a large number were written for the *United States Literary Gazette*, and the various magazines he edited in New York. When he became editor of the *Evening Post* he continued to edit the *United States Review and Literary Gazette*, until it was discontinued. After

that he assisted in editing an annual called *The
Talisman*, which appeared regularly until 1829.
To this he contributed a considerable number of
poems. But now for several years he wrote but
little poetry, giving all his time and energy to the
newspaper.

In 1831, however, he published a second collection of his poems. There were eighty in the
volume. Then he thought he would see how
they would be received in England. He had a
friend who knew Washington Irving. Irving was
a famous writer at this time, and his publisher was
John Murray, one of the greatest of English publishers. Bryant obtained an introduction to Irving
by letter, and asked him to assist in getting Murray to bring out a London edition of his poems.
Murray would not do it, however. But Irving
admired Bryant's work, and after a time he found
another publisher who was willing to bring out the
volume. He himself wrote an introduction, and
dedicated the book to Rogers, the fashionable poet
of England at that time. But before the book
came out the publisher, a fussy old man, came to

Irving and said it would never do to print in England the line,

And the British foeman trembles.

That would be sure to offend the stolid Briton's pride. So Irving changed the line to

The foeman trembles in his camp.

Years afterward there was some controversy over this change on the part of Irving ; but Irving and Bryant always remained good friends.

Other volumes of his collected poems were published from time to time after this ; but they are not important. The only other great poetic work that Bryant attempted was his translation of Homer's Iliad and Odyssey. When he translated these grand Greek poems into English blank verse he was already quite an old man. His wife had died, and he wished some regular work, aside from his paper, that would claim his thoughts. So he made it a practice to translate a few lines every day. This he kept up for a number of years, until he had translated the whole of both these long poems.

For this he probably received more money than

for all his other poems put together—over seventeen thousand dollars in all.

We must next speak of his travels; for Bryant was a great traveler. His first long journey was made in 1832 to visit his brothers, who had become the proprietors of a large landed estate in Illinois. He was three weeks on the journey out. While crossing the prairies between the Mississippi River and his brothers' plantation he met a company of Illinois volunteers, who were going to take part in the Black Hawk War. They were led by a tall, awkward, uncouth lad, whose appearance attracted Bryant's attention, and whose conversation pleased him, it was so breezy and original. He learned many years afterward that this captain was Abraham Lincoln. When in 1860 it was proposed to nominate Lincoln for President, Lincoln came to New York to speak, and Bryant introduced him to the audience.

It was during his visit to his brothers that he wrote of

> The unshorn fields, boundless and beautiful,
> For which the speech of England has no name.

He evidently liked the West, for we have seen that later he proposed to sell out his paper and go there to live.

In 1834 he made his first trip to Europe. While he was gone he wrote letters regularly for his paper ; but he traveled leisurely and enjoyed himself. He took his wife and daughters with him. He remained two years, when he was called home by the illness of the associate editor, who had charge of the paper in his absence.

After this, at various times, he visited Europe again, crossing the Atlantic in all six times. One of these journeys, made in 1857, was chiefly for Mrs. Bryant's health. They landed at Havre, and journeyed through Belgium and Holland, France and Spain to Madrid, whence they crossed to Naples, where Mrs. Bryant was ill for four months. She recovered somewhat, but when at last they returned to the United States she was not much better. Bryant had bought the old homestead at Cummington, and had invited all his relatives from Illinois to join him in "hanging the pot." In July, 1858, he had to notify his brothers, some of whom were already at Cummington, that his wife was too ill to go there ; and on the 27th of that month she died. In regard to her death he wrote to a friend, "I lived with my wife forty-five years, and now that great blessing of my life is withdrawn, and I am like one cast out of paradise and wandering in a strange world."

Nearly ten years before this, in 1849, he made a visit of two months to Cuba, going by way of the Carolinas and Florida. He was "received by the governor-general of Havana, and passed several days on a coffee estate at Matanzas, going then by rail to San Antonio in a car built at Newark, drawn by an engine made in New York, and worked by an American engineer. He breakfasted at the inn of La Punta on rice and fresh eggs and a dish of meat. He witnessed a cock-fight, a masked ball, a murderer garroted, and slavery in some of its most inhuman phases."

He also visited Mexico, Egypt, and the Shetland Islands, and was everywhere an interested observer of men and manners.

CHAPTER XII

HONORS TO THE GREAT POET

We have seen that Bryant was not only a great poet, but a great newspaper editor, an eloquent orator, and a rich man. So he came to be a noted public character, one of the leading citizens of the great city of New York. From this time forward until his death in extreme old age, prominent statesmen, politicians, poets, people of society, hastened to shower honors upon him. He was asked to be a regent of the University of New York, but declined. Banquets were also tendered him, which he also declined. But on his seventieth birthday, November 3, 1864, the Century Club of New York, of which he had been one of the founders, resolved to make a great festival in his honor. Bancroft, the historian, was president of the club, and greeted Bryant with a graceful speech on that great occasion. In Bryant's reply is the following passage, which will be of interest to all young people as showing that this great and wise man believed in placing responsibility on the young, and not in keeping them in the background for wise old heads.

"Much has been said of the wisdom of Old Age," said he. "Old Age is wise, I grant, for itself, but not wise for the community. It is wise in declining new enterprises, for it has not the power nor the time to execute them ; wise in shirking from difficulty, for it has not the strength to overcome it ; wise in avoiding danger, for it lacks the faculty of ready and swift action, by which dangers are parried and converted into advantages. But this is not wisdom for mankind at large, by whom new enterprises must be undertaken, dangers met, and difficulties surmounted. What a world this would be if it were made up of old men !"

Oliver Wendell Holmes was there, and read a beautiful poem composed for the occasion. There were also other poems read by their authors, and Whittier and Lowell, who could not be there, sent their poems to be read, while Longfellow and a great many other famous people wrote letters of congratulation.

Here are some of the beautiful lines from the poem which Dr. Holmes read :

How can we praise the verse whose music flows
With solemn cadence and majestic close,
Pure as the dew that filters through the rose?

How shall we thank him that in evil days
He faltered never,—nor for blame. nor praise,
Nor hire nor party, shared his earlier days ?

But as his boyhood was of manliest hue,
So to his youth his manly years were true,
All dyed in royal purple through and through.

Ralph Waldo Emerson was there, and made a speech, which he closed with this verse, written by the poet Crabbe :

True bard, and simple as the race
Of heaven-born poets always are,
When stooping from their starry place
They're children near but gods afar.

This means that great poets seem very great and magnificent when we think of them after they are dead and gone, or when they live by themselves at a great distance ; but really, when you know them, they are as natural and human as children. That perfectly describes William Cullen Bryant.

In 1874 Bryant was elected an honorary member of the Russian Academy of St. Petersburg. The same year, on his eightieth birthday, he was presented with an address of honor, signed by thousands and thousands of people. This was accompanied by a special vase, completed sometime afterward, which commemorated his literary career. A little later in the same year he visited Governor Tilden at Albany, and was tendered a public reception. After that some of his friends proposed that he should be nominated as one of the electors on the Tilden electoral ticket, when Tilden was a candidate for the presidency of the United States.

These and many other public honors were heaped upon him in his old age. When over eighty-three years of age he was invited to deliver an address on the unveiling of a statue of Mazzini, the Italian patriot, in Central Park, New York City. After it was over, he was very much exhausted, but walked across the park to the house of a friend. On the steps he fell, being old and feeble and very tired. His head hit on a stone and he fainted away. Less than two weeks later, June 12, 1878, he died from the effects of this fall.

CHAPTER XIII

LEARNING TO LOVE A POET

It is not uncommon to hear young people say, "I don't like poetry at all. It is dry, horrid stuff, and I don't understand it." No doubt some of you will say or think this about Bryant's poetry. It is true that he used a great many long, hard words; and his poems are sometimes rather solemn. What is more, they are not musical like Longfellow's. It is said that Bryant had no ear for music. For this reason you cannot read his poetry as you do Longfellow's, swinging along from line to line. Young people who read in the sing-song style will find that they cannot do that when they come to Bryant. At first you may think his poetry is, for this reason, not good poetry at all. Perhaps it

would be better to call Bryant a prose poet instead
of a musical poet.   But when you get used to his
prose-like poetry, you will like it if you have in
you the least love of nature or natural beauty.

Take some one poem that you like and read it
over and over again, until you have it almost if not
quite by heart—for instance, that beautiful poem,
"The Death of the Flowers," written on the occasion of his sister's death :

The melancholy days are come, the saddest of the
   year,
Of wailing winds, and naked woods, and meadows brown
   and sere.
Heaped in the hollows of the grove, the autumn leaves
   lie dead;
They rustle to the eddying gust, and to the rabbit's
   tread.
The robin and the wren are flown, and from the shrubs
   the jay,
And from the wood-top calls the crow through all the
   gloomy day.

Other poems that are well worth reading many
times, until you really understand and love them,
are "The Waterfowl," "Autumn Woods," "No-

vember," "The Gladness of Nature," "The
Past," "To the Fringed Gentian," "The Con-
queror's Grave," "An Invitation to the Country,"
"The Wind and the Stream," "The Poet,"
"May Evening," "The Flood of Years," and
"Our Fellow-Worshipers." To have mastered
one of these poems is better than to have read the
whole of Bryant carelessly. Take one, and read
it until by very force of habit you learn to love it;
and then the next poem you take up will reveal
beauties which you never suspected when you
first read it.

There is also a city poem of Bryant's, "The
Crowded Street," well worth learning to love:

> Let me move slowly through the street,
>   Filled with an ever-shifting train,
> Amid the sound of steps that beat
>   The murmuring walks like autumn rain.
>
> How fast the flitting figures come!
>   The mild, the fierce, the stony face;
> Some bright with thoughtless smiles, and some
>   Where secret tears have left their trace.

And here is one more short poem, which may you

all remember, long after you have forgotten that
you ever read this little history of the poet's life!

THE DEATH OF LINCOLN.

Oh, slow to smite and swift to spare,
　Gentle and merciful and just!
Who, in the fear of God, didst bear
　The sword of power, a nation's trust!

In sorrow by thy bier we stand,
　Amid the awe that hushes all,
And speak the anguish of a land
　That shook with horror at thy fall.

Thy task is done; the bond are free:
　We bear thee to an honored grave,
Whose proudest monument shall be
　The broken fetters of the slave.

Pure was thy life; its bloody close
　Hath placed thee with the sons of light,
Among the noblest host of those
　Who perished in the cause of Right.

THE STORY OF
HENRY W. LONGFELLOW

HENRY WADSWORTH LONGFELLOW

LONGFELLOW

CHAPTER I

A GREAT POET

Lives of great men all remind us
  We can make our lives sublime,
And, departing, leave behind us
  Footprints on the sands of time;—

Footprints, that perhaps another,
  Saïling o'er life's solemn main,
A forlorn and shipwrecked brother,
  Seeing, shall take heart again.

You doubtless remember how Robinson Crusoe one day found footprints in the sand on the shore of his desert island. "I am not alone!" said he to himself. "Another human being has been here before me." Soon afterward he had the good fortune to find his "man Friday."

In geology we learn of footprints in rocks. Living beings ages ago walked on the soft sand, and that sand, lying for a long time undisturbed, was at length hardened into rock.

The poet Longfellow has left "footprints on the sands of time" in the shape of his poems, and we may say those poems are like footprints hardened into rock, which will last for ages. Many an unhappy soul, after reading the sad, sweet, beautiful verses of the "Psalm of Life," has taken heart to go on fighting life's battle nobly, and doing good instead of yielding to the temptation to be weak and careless.

To realize what it is to be a great poet, think of the millions of boys and girls, old and young, in the United States, and in Great Britain and other foreign countries, who have learned by heart such famous poems as "The Village Blacksmith," "The Wreck of the Hesperus," and "The Building of the Ship." You, yourself, no doubt, dear reader, when you want something to memorize, turn to a volume of Longfellow's poems. You have learned to love the poems: therefore let me introduce to you the man who first lived the poems in his own life, and you will certainly learn to love him, too.

The poet was born February 27, 1807, in Portland, Maine. At the time of his birth his parents were living in Captain Stephenson's house, Mrs. Stephenson being a sister of the elder Mr. Longfellow. But this was only temporarily, indeed only while the Stephenson family were visiting the West Indies. The Longfellows soon moved into the house of General Peleg Wadsworth, where Mrs. Longfellow had spent part of her girlhood. It is said to have been the first brick house ever built in Portland, and it was one of the finest. Here they lived until the baby grew into a man.

CHAPTER II

LONGFELLOW'S ANCESTORS

Henry Wadsworth Longfellow belonged to a good old New England family. His father was a lawyer in Portland, Maine; his grandfather had been a schoolmaster; and his great-grandfather had been a blacksmith.

The Longfellows were most of them tall, strong men, who had been soldiers, sailors and the like, and none of them had shown the slightest talent for poetry. But Henry Wadsworth Longfellow was small and delicate, though he always stood very erect and was a finely formed man.

His grandfather on his mother's side was General Peleg Wadsworth, who was once captured by the British and came near being shipped off to England; but he escaped and joined his wife and family as they were going to Boston. The poet also had an uncle Henry (for whom he was named), who had been a lieutenant with Commodore Preble and was killed at Tripoli a short time before his namesake was born. Another uncle was a second lieutenant on the frigate *Constitution* when it captured the British ship *Guerrière* in 1812.

On his mother's side, Longfellow could trace his origin straight back to John Alden and Priscilla Mullens, who came over in the *Mayflower*, and whom he has made immortal in his poem of "The Courtship of Miles Standish."

In short, Longfellow belonged to quite an aristocratic family, as New England aristocracy goes, and it was a fairly wealthy family also. His father was once a member of Congress, and afterward was chosen to make the speech welcoming Lafayette when he visited Portland in 1825.

The house where Longfellow was born is still standing and is well known to the children of Portland. In the old days it was in the fashionable part of the town, facing the ocean beach. But now land has been filled in for a long distance out into the ocean, and on this new land stand the engine-house and tracks of the Grand Trunk railway. So the house is now in a very poor neighborhood.

One day a teacher in a Portland school asked her pupils if they knew where Longfellow was born.

"I know," said a little girl. "In Patsey Connor's bedroom."

Many poor people lived in the house, and the room where Longfellow was born was now Patsey Connor's bedroom; but all the children of Portland knew where it was.

CHAPTER III

LONGFELLOW'S BOYHOOD

Our poet seems to have been a quiet, well behaved child, rather slight, but always standing up perfectly straight. He was careful of his clothes, and learned his lessons well. Some people seem to think that a very good little boy will never grow up to be worth anything. Certainly it is a good thing to have plenty of spirit and energy; but Longfellow is an example of a boy who was as good as George Washington is said to have been, and he grew up to be the greatest poet in America, just as Washington grew up to be the greatest president.

When he was three years old little Henry was sent to school. For a good many years a certain Ma'am Fellows had kept a school in a little brick schoolhouse not far from the Wadsworth mansion, and it was she who taught the poet his first lessons. Ma'am Fellows was a firm believer in the doctrine that "one should never smile in school hours." Years afterward Longfellow told what he remembered of her. "My recollections of my first teacher," said the poet, "are not vivid: but I recall that she was bent on giving me a right start in life; that she thought that even very young children should be made to know the difference between right and wrong; and that severity of manner was more practical than gentleness of persuasion. She inspired me with one trait,—that is, a genuine respect for my elders."

He afterward went to several other schools, including one in Love Lane. When he grew a little older he had to write compositions, and there is a story about the first one he ever wrote. His teacher told him to write a composition; but he thought he couldn't do it.

"But you can write words, can you not?" asked the teacher.

"Yes," was the response.

"Then you can put words together?"

"Yes, sir."

"Then," said the instructor, "you may take your slate and go out behind the schoolhouse, and there you can find something to write about; and then you can tell what it is, what it is for, and what is to be done with it; and that will be a composition."

Henry took his slate and went out. He went behind Mr. Finney's barn, which chanced to be near; and, seeing a fine turnip growing, he thought he knew what it was, what it was for, and what would be done with it.

A half hour had been allowed young Henry for his first undertaking in writing compositions. Before that time had expired he carried in his work, very neatly written on his slate. It was so well done that his teacher was both surprised and pleased.

There has been published in the newspapers a very funny poem about a turnip, and some have said that it is the one which Longfellow wrote at this time. But the truth is, he never wrote it, for that first composition was rubbed off the slate and lost forever. This other poem was written years afterward by somebody for a joke. Here is the poem, however, for you to laugh about. You will clearly see that Longfellow could not have written it himself.

MR. FINNEY'S TURNIP

Mr. Finney had a turnip,
  And it grew, and it grew;
And it grew behind the barn,
  And the turnip did no harm.

And it grew and it grew,
  Till it could grow no taller;
Then Mr. Finney took it up,
  And put it in the cellar.

There it lay, there it lay,
  Till it began to rot;
When his daughter Susie washed it,
  And put it in the pot.

Then she boiled it, and she boiled it,
  As long as she was able;
Then his daughter Lizzie took it,
  And she put it on the table.

Mr. Finney and his wife
  Both sat down to sup;
And they ate, and they ate,
  Until they ate the turnip up.

When he was only thirteen years old Longfellow
wrote a real poem, which, though it has never been

published, is said to have been preserved in manuscript. It was entitled "Venice, an Italian Song." The manuscript is dated "Portland Academy, March 17, 1820," and is signed with the full name of the writer.

It was not long after this that his first published poem appeared. It was entitled "The Battle of Lovell's Pond," and was printed in one of the newspapers of Portland.

There were only two papers in that city then. Having written the ballad very carefully and neatly, Henry thought he would like to see it in print; but he was afraid to take it to the editor. One of his school-mates persuaded him, however, and he stole up one night and dropped it into the editorial box.

He waited patiently for the next issue of the paper, and then scanned its columns for his poem, which he thought surely would be there. But it wasn't. Many weeks passed and it did not appear. At last he went and asked to have his manuscript returned.

It was given him and he took it over to the other

paper, the *Portland Gazette*, by whose editor it was accepted and immediately published over the signature '' Henry." Here are the first two stanzas:

Cold, cold is the north wind and rude is the blast
That sweeps like a hurricane loudly and fast,
As it moans through the tall waving pines, lone and drear,
Sighs a requiem sad o'er the warrior's bier.

The war-whoop is still, and the savage's yell
Has sunk into silence along the wild dell;
The din of the battle, the tumult is o'er,
And the war-clarion's voice is now heard no more.

After that the young poet could have his verses printed in that paper as often as he liked, and he wrote a number of pieces for this purpose.

He went to Portland Academy, and was ready to enter college at fourteen. One of his teachers at the academy, who, no doubt, did a great deal to impress his young mind, was Jacob Abbott, the author of the ''Rollo Books." Some years ago these were the most popular books for boys and girls then known, and perhaps some of the young people of this generation have read them. If they have, they will know what fine books they are.

CHAPTER IV

SOMETHING ABOUT THE TIMES WHEN LONGFELLOW WAS YOUNG

In the days when Longfellow was a child, people were just changing from the old fashioned style of living to ways that were new and more modern. The older men wore knee breeches and silk stockings, and shoes with big buckles, and had their long hair gathered in a knot or "club" behind.

Those were strict Puritan days, too. Everybody was very careful about going to church and keeping Sunday, and theaters were prohibited until a few years later. They do say, however, that the people drank a good deal of Jamaica rum and did other things that we should not approve of to-day.

Portland was quite a seaport, and had formerly enjoyed great business prosperity. But in the year that Longfellow was born, the embargo was put on shipping, and severe "hard times" came on. It is said "the grass literally grew upon the wharves."

Five years after his birth, came the war of 1812.

Fortifications were thrown up on Munjoy's Hill, and privateers were fitted out in the harbor. In his beautiful poem, "My Lost Youth," Longfellow refers to this.

This poem is very interesting when we think of the actual places to which Longfellow refers. Of course he is thinking of Portland when he writes:

> Often I think of the beautiful town
>   That is seated by the sea;
>
> *   *   *   *   *   *
>
> I can see the shadowy lines of its trees,
>   And catch, in sudden gleams,
> The sheen of the far-surrounding seas,
> And islands that were the Hesperides
>   Of all my boyish dreams.
>
> *   *   *   *   *   *
>
> I remember the black wharves and the slips,
>   And the sea-tides tossing free;
> And Spanish sailors with bearded lips,
> And the beauty and mystery of the ships,
>   And the magic of the sea.

In the following lines he refers to the fortifications that were put up when he was five years old:

> I remember the bulwarks by the shore,
>   And the fort upon the hill;
> The sunrise gun, with its hollow roar,
> The drum-beat repeated o'er and o'er.
>   And the bugle wild and shrill.

On the 4th of September, 1813, the *Boxer*, British brig of war, was captured off the Maine coast by the American brig *Enterprise*, and a few days later was brought into Portland harbor. On the next day both commanders, who had been killed in the encounter, were buried in the cemetery at the foot of Munjoy's Hill. The poet thus records his recollections of that event:

> I remember the sea-fight far away,
>   How it thundered o'er the tide!
> And the dead captains, as they lay
> In their graves, o'erlooking the tranquil bay,
>   Where they in battle died.

While referring to this poem, it may be noted that Longfellow was very fond of the country, as well as of the sea, and he never lived in a city larger than Cambridge, which is really no city at all, but merely a college town. Near his home in

Portland was a large piece of woodland where he
was very fond of roaming about with some of his
friends. He thus speaks of it in the poem:

> I can see the breezy dome of groves,
>   The shadows of Deering's Woods;
> And the friendships old and the early loves
> Come back with a sabbath sound, as of doves
>   In quiet neighborhoods.
>
>   * * * * * *
>
> I remember the gleams and glooms that dart
>   Across the schoolboy's brain;
> The song and the silence in the heart,
> That in part are prophecies, and in part
>   Are longings wild and vain.

At the end of each verse comes the beautiful
refrain—

> And the voice of that fitful song
> Sings on, and is never still:
> "A boy's will is the wind's will,
> And the thoughts of youth are long, long thoughts."

Several other poems were suggested by the
sights and sounds of the poet's boyhood. One was
"The Ropewalk," describing a building that he

often passed. There was also a factory where crude pottery was made and where he went and watched the turning wheel that suggested to him many years later the beautiful poem entitled '' Keramos."

CHAPTER V

COLLEGE DAYS

Longfellow went to college when he was very young, indeed only fourteen years old. In those days the requirements for entering college were not so severe as they are now; yet they were by no means easy, and only a bright scholar could pass the examinations. Longfellow was one of the bright boys. He stood second in his class. He had an elder brother, Stephen, who entered college at that same time.

His father and grandfather were graduates of Harvard College; but as his father was then a trustee of Bowdoin College, at Brunswick, Maine, he was sent there. It happened that in the class which he entered there were several other youths who became very famous men. One was Hawthorne, the greatest American novelist; and in the class just above was Franklin Pierce, who afterwards became President of the United States. Not quite so famous as these two was another classmate of Longfellow's, John S. C. Abbott, whose histories for young people have been only less popular than the "Rollo Books" written by his brother, Jacob Abbott, a somewhat older man.

In those days no one suspected that there were in that college men destined to become so great. Longfellow was merely an aristocratic young man who stood well in his classes and "wrote verses as a pastime." The poet of the class was a young man named Mellen. Hawthorne was very shy and never learned his lessons. He studied in his own way, and his professors had a very good opinion of him, but he was not a good scholar.

There were in college two different kinds of students, the country boys and the city fellows. The country boys were usually rough, brown, and not very well dressed. They would lumber along

the streets like farmers, as they were. It may
easily be imagined that they were not rich. The
lads from the seaports, on the other hand, the
city fellows, had white hands and faces, were fash-
ionably dressed, and were usually considered rich.

Longfellow was a city lad, and had plenty of
money. Hawthorne was more of a country fellow.
While in college the two were not intimate. Both
were naturally modest and shy, and each had only
a few friends with whom he associated. But some
years after they left college, Hawthorne sent his
first volume of stories, the "Twice-told Tales," to
Longfellow, then a professor at Harvard College,
and Longfellow wrote a very kind article about it,
which was published in the *North American Review.*
It was the first worthy recognition Hawthorne had
received, and he was very grateful to Longfellow.
This made them warm friends, and such they
remained for the rest of their lives.

During his first year Longfellow did most of his
studying at home. He was doubtless a little home-
sick at Brunswick, at first. That town is not very
far from Portland, but it took some time to get

there, for in those days there were no railroads. The two Longfellow boys went up the coast in a sailing boat to a town not far from Brunswick, and from there they went by stage.

While in college young Henry had no great adventures. He was a well behaved young man, never hazed anybody, and was generally thought rather a good fellow, but not remarkable in any way. He wrote a good deal of poetry, which was printed in the *United States Literary Gazette*, without his name; but his cousin John Owen, then at college with him, told him to his face one day that poetry was not his forte.

One other thing remains to be said of his college life. Though rich, he was generous toward his poorer classmates, and at the same time very modest and quiet about it. Here is one case, and there are a good many others.

There was a student who had worked hard to finish his college course; but one day he received word that owing to the death of his father he would have to leave college and earn his own living; the family could spare him no more money to help him through. This was sad news to him, for he had great ambitions and hopes concerning his future career.

A friend of his, belonging to the class below Longfellow's, went to the poet and asked him if he would not head a subscription, or do something of the kind. At this time the poet had been contributing pretty regularly to the *United States Literary Gazette*, and had never received any pay for it. Many of the poems had been copied in the daily and weekly papers.

He wrote a note to the editor saying that he thought he deserved in the future to be paid for his contributions. His intention was to give the money to his college mate. But the editor replied that poems were generally printed gratis, and made some vague promises.

This was a disappointment; but the classmate who tells the story, Longfellow, and his brother Stephen drew up a subscription paper, put down such sums as they could afford, and passed the document about among the college men. Enough money was raised to carry the poor fellow through his college course.

"For some reason or other," says his cousin John Owen, "the poet never liked to speak of this act of his earlier career. He and I have talked about it, to be sure; but one day he suggested that the subject be forever dropped. It was one of his peculiar habits—always to be doing some one a favor, and to wish that it be kept a profound secret."

CHAPTER VI

THE YOUNG PROFESSOR

When Longfellow graduated from college he was a young man of nineteen, slender, well built, and graceful. He had blue eyes and light-brown hair which he wore rather heavy about his head. In his dress he was somewhat fastidious, and afterward certain people were inclined to make fun of his variety of neckties and light vests. But he always showed the best of taste.

His father wished him to be a lawyer. But in the year that he graduated a new professorship was founded at Bowdoin, the professorship of · modern languages, and he was chosen to fill it. Before that, Latin and Greek had been considered the only languages worth studying. · But French, German, Italian, and Spanish were demanding attention.

The story is that, while a student in college, Longfellow had written a metrical translation of one of Horace's odes, which he had read at a general examination. One of the examiners, the Hon. Benjamin Orr, a distinguished lawyer of Maine, was greatly struck with this translation, which seemed to him especially beautiful. He was one of the board of trustees, and when the new professorship was created he nominated the future poet, speaking of this translation as evidence of his ability to fill the position.

Longfellow was only nineteen years old, and the proposition came to him as a great surprise. As a preparation he was to be allowed to spend three years in Europe. By this time he was anxious to enter a literary career, and this seemed to be just the chance. His father consented and he prepared to set out for Europe, though he did not start until the following spring.

What his experiences were abroad, you may learn by reading "Outre-Mer." This book · is partly a story, but in reality it describes Longfellow's journeyings through Germany, France, Italy, and Spain. He went from New York on a slow sailing vessel; but his trip was a pleasant one, and he seemed always to be lucky, as he was through life.

At last, at twenty-two, he found himself a professor in Bòwdoin College, and quite a distinguished young man. His "April Day" and "Woods in Winter," two short poems, had been copied in many newspapers, and had even got into the reading books of that day. His name was not attached to any of these, and no one thought of him as a great poet. It must be remembered that teaching was hereafter the business of his life; and a very faithful teacher he was. Up to this time, and for long afterward, he did not receive any money whatever for his poetry, though occasionally some was promised him.

He studied very hard. He knew German thoroughly well, and also French, Italian, Spanish, Swedish, Finnish, and even something of other modern languages. In those days people knew very little about these languages, and few supposed they had literature that was worth anything. Longfellow became a great scholar in them, however, and translated poetry from nearly all of them. If you look in his complete works you will find a great many poems marked as translations from German, or Spanish, or Swedish, or some other language. Many of these were printed in learned essays which he wrote and published in the *North American Review.*

He was very popular as a teacher. He seemed to the boys like one of themselves, and he was very sympathetic with them. Yet they all respected him, and treated him politely. They thought that he would some time be a famous man, and yet it seemed more as if he would be a great scholar, than a popular poet whom everybody, boys and girls as well as grown-up people, could understand and like.

CHAPTER VII

THE "BEING BEAUTEOUS"

When he had been a professor at Bowdoin College but little over a year, Longfellow married a young lady named Mary Storer Potter. She was the daughter of a well-known judge who lived in Portland, and was something of a scholar too. It is said she was especially fond of mathematics, and had been taught to calculate eclipses. In those days girls were sent to school very little, and none of them ever went to college. The old Puritan fathers thought girls were better off at home doing housework. But Longfellow's wife was more fortunate.

She was at the same time good-looking and very pleasant to every one, and so the young professor and his young wife were invited about a great deal, and everybody thought them a very happy pair.

They were very happy together for two or three years; then Longfellow was asked to go to Harvard College to be professor of modern languages there. To prepare for this new and more prominent position he went to Europe again. Of course his wife went with him. They traveled about for some time; but she was not well, and finally she died.

Most of the poem entitled "Footsteps of Angels" is about her, and it shows just what he thought of her. It is worth remembering that this is the poet's own real wife who died when they were both quite young. Here is a part of the poem. The last stanzas refer to her.

> When the hours of day are numbered,
>   And the voices of the Night
> Wake the better soul, that slumbered,
>   To a holy, calm delight;
>
> Ere the evening lamps are lighted,
>   And, like phantoms grim and tall,
> Shadows from the fitful firelight
>   Dance upon the parlor wall;
>
> Then the forms of the departed
>   Enter at the open door;
> The beloved, the true-hearted,
>   Come to visit me once more;
> *   *   *   *   *   *

And with them the Being Beauteous,
　Who unto my youth was given,
More than all things else to love me,
　And is now a saint in heaven.

With a slow and noiseless footstep
　Comes that messenger divine,
Takes the vacant chair beside me,
　Lays her gentle hand in mine.

And she sits and gazes at me,
　With those deep and tender eyes,
Like the stars, so still and saint-like,
　Looking downward from the skies.

Uttered not, yet comprehended,
　Is the spirit's voiceless prayer,
Soft rebukes, in blessings ended,
　Breathing from her lips of air.

Oh, though oft depressed and lonely,
　All my fears are laid aside,
If I but remember only
　Such as these have lived and died!

CHAPTER VIII

THE CRAIGIE HOUSE

Longfellow came back from Europe and was installed as professor of modern languages and belles-lettres at Harvard College, in the beautiful town of Cambridge, two miles from Boston. Soon after he began his life there he went to live at the Craigie House, which has become so famous as the home of Longfellow that it deserves a little description.

It will be remembered that Longfellow was now a widower without children, his wife having died during his second journey to Europe. When he came to settle in Cambridge he was attracted by the spacious rooms and the quiet and aristocratic air of the Craigie House, famous as the headquarters of Washington when he was in Cambridge as commander-in-chief during the Revolutionary War. George William Curtis has told the story of Longfellow's first visit to this house and how he came to live there, and we give it here very nearly in Mr. Curtis's own words.

In the summer of 1837, a young man passed down the elm-shaded walk that separated the old Craigie House from the high road. Reaching the door he paused to observe the huge old-fashioned brass knocker and the quaint handle, relics, evidently, of an epoch of colonial state. To his mind, however, the house, and these signs of its age, were not interesting from the romance of antiquity alone, but from their association with the early days of our Revolution, when General Washington, after the battle of Bunker Hill, had his headquarters in the mansion. Had his hand, perhaps, lifted the same latch, lingering, as he pressed it, in a whirl of myriad emotions? Had he, too, paused in the calm summer afternoon, and watched the silver gleam of the broad river in the meadows, the dreamy blue of the Milton hills beyond? And had the tranquillity of that landscape penetrated his heart with "the sleep that is among the hills," and whose fairest dream to him was a hope now realized in the peaceful prosperity of his country?

He was ushered in and found himself face to face with Mrs. Craigie, a good old lady who had seen better days. He asked if there was a room vacant in the house.

"I lodge no students," was her reply. Longfellow was so young-looking she took him to be a student.

"I am not a student," answered the visitor, "but a professor in the university."

"A professor?" she inquired. She thought a professor ought to be dressed like a clergyman.

"Professor Longfellow," continued the guest, introducing himself.

"Ah! that is different," said the lady, her features slightly relaxing, as if professors were naturally harmless and she need no longer barricade herself behind a stern gravity of demeanor. "I will show you what there is."

She preceded the professor upstairs, and going down the hall she stopped at each door, opened it, permitted him to perceive its delightful fitness for his purpose, then quietly closed the door, observing, "You cannot have that." The professorial eyes glanced restlessly around the fine old-fashioned points of the mansion, marked the wooden carvings, the air of opulent respectability in the past, which corresponds in New England to the impression of ancient nobility in Old England, and wondered if he were not to be permitted to have a room at all. The old lady at length opened the door of the southeast corner room in the second story; and while the guest looked wistfully in and awaited the customary "You cannot have that," he was agreeably surprised by hearing that he might have it.

The room was upon the front of the house and overlooked the meadows to the river. It had an atmosphere of fascinating repose, in which the young man at once felt at home.

"This," said the lady, "was Washington's chamber."

Here Longfellow lived for the rest of his life. He was merely a lodger in one of the rooms until he married the second time, six years after first going there. On his marriage his wife's father, Mr. Nathan Appleton, who was a rich old gentleman, bought the house and gave it to him as a wedding present, and also gave him the lot opposite, so that no one should ever build a house that would shut off his view of the river Charles.

It was the view from the front of this house that inspired the poet to write that beautiful poem, ''To the River Charles.'' How sweet and suggestive the opening verses, which note that he wrote the poem four years after he moved into the Craigie House!

> River! that in silence windest
> Through the meadows, bright and free,
> Till at length thy rest thou findest
> In the bosom of the sea!
>
> Four long years of mingled feeling,
> Half in rest, and half in strife,
> I have seen thy waters stealing
> Onward, like the stream of life.
>
> Thou hast taught me, Silent River!
> Many a lesson, deep and long;
> Thou hast been a generous giver;
> I can give thee but a song.

It may be said that Joseph Worcester, who wrote Worcester's Dictionary, had once lived in this house, and Miss Sally Lowell, an aunt of

James Russell Lowell, as well as Jared Sparks, who wrote a great life of Washington and was president of Harvard College. Mr. Sparks and Edward Everett both brought their wives there when they were married.

It seemed that Longfellow was always getting into famous houses. When he was at Bowdoin College he lived in the house in which "Uncle Tom's Cabin" was afterward written. It is said that Talleyrand, the famous French diplomat, and the Duke of Kent, Queen Victoria's father, had been entertained at dinner at the Craigie House when it belonged to the original owner, Colonel John Vassal.

CHAPTER IX

THE FIVE OF CLUBS

Now began the finest years of Longfellow's life. It was in the early years at the Craigie House that he wrote the "Psalm of Life" and most of his other world-famous and world-loved poems, and it was here that he enjoyed his best friendships.

When he first came to Cambridge to see about accepting the professorship, he was introduced to Charles Sumner, the great lawyer, orator, and statesman, then a young man beginning to practice law in Boston. The introduction took place in Professor Felton's rooms, who was also about the same age, that is, under thirty, and who as a Greek scholar and the writer of Greek textbooks has become famous. Felton was a big, good-natured fellow; and he and Charles Sumner at once took a fancy to Longfellow. As soon as the poet was settled in his new home a club was formed, consisting of Longfellow, Sumner, Felton, George S. Hillard (Sumner's law partner), and Henry R. Cleveland, who was also a teacher. These five, who called themselves "The Five of Clubs," met usually every Saturday afternoon in Longfellow's room, sometimes in Felton's, and occasionally in the law offices of Sumner and Hillard in Boston. They were all ambitious, all good fellows who met for a "feast of reason," but who nevertheless knew how to have a royal good time. These meetings were kept up regularly for several years.

It was about this time that Longfellow's friendship for Hawthorne began.

There were many other famous people here, too, with whom Longfellow formed life-long friendships. Holmes was becoming known as a young poet as well as medical professor in Harvard College, and Lowell, then a boy, was soon to come upon the scene, and at last to take Longfellow's professorship when Longfellow should resign.

Charles Sumner was destined to be one of the great antislavery agitators, and it was chiefly to his influence that we owe Longfellow's poems on slavery. Longfellow was not of a very fiery nature. He did not get excited even in those hot times before the war, and Sumner had to urge him a long time before he composed the poems entitled "The Slave's Dream," "The Slave in the Dismal Swamp," and others on slavery.

Emerson was also one of his friends, and so were several others among those who started the Brook Farm experiment. These people had taken a farm, and all had gone to live together on it, each doing a little work, and all doing a great deal of talking. Some of Emerson's friends rather disliked Longfellow because he took no interest in this scheme, which proved a terrible failure. While he was intimate with the Brook Farm people, and always friendly as far as listening to them was concerned, he kept on the even tenor of his ways quite unmoved by their arguments.

CHAPTER X

LONGFELLOW BECOMES A FAMOUS POET

When Longfellow went to live in Cambridge he was just thirty years old. He had not then written any of the poems that are famous to-day, but he began at once to produce most of those that we love best. A good many of them were sent to the *Knickerbocker Magazine*. One of them was the "Psalm of Life," for which he was promised five dollars, which, however, was never paid him. A poem then called "Floral Astrology," but now known as "Flowers," was the first to have his full name attached—"Harvard College, H. W. Long-fellow." The "Psalm of Life" was signed sim-ply "L." Both of these poems and "The Reaper and the Flowers" (published in the same magazine in the same way, at the same price, which was never paid) had been copied into hundreds of news-papers and were public favorites without the author's being in the least known. His friends knew Longfellow wrote the poems, but the public did not.

His cousin, John Owen, kept a bookstore in Cambridge. One day Owen went to him and told him he ought to have some of his poems printed in a little volume, and with his name. Longfellow objected to having his name appear, though he thought it might be a good idea to have the poems published if a publisher could be found. His cousin said he should like to publish them; to this Longfellow assented, but for some time refused to have his name appear. At last he said, "Well, bring them out in your own way!" That meant, with his name on the title page.

That little volume, entitled "Voices of the

Night," and including the poems still printed in Longfellow's collected works under that title, was published in 1839, when Longfellow was thirty-two years old. It contained the "Psalm of Life," "The Reaper and the Flowers," "The Light of Stars," "Footsteps of Angels," "Flowers," "The Beleaguered City," and "Midnight Mass to the Dying Year." There were also some translations, and a few of the poems he had published while in college.

That book made Longfellow famous as a poet. A few critics found fault with it, but not many, and hundreds of others liked it and praised it. Longfellow himself tells a pretty story of the "Psalm of Life." "I was once riding in London," said he, "when a laborer approached the carriage and asked, 'Are you the writer of the "Psalm of Life?"' 'I am.' 'Will you allow me to shake hands with you?' We clasped hands warmly. The carriage passed on, and I saw him no more; but I remember that as one of the most gratifying compliments I ever received, because it was so sincere."

In a published letter from Charles Sumner, there is another touching story of the power this wonderful poem possesses over men.

A man who had been very unlucky, an old classmate of Sumner's, went to his office to prove some debts in bankruptcy. Sumner asked him what he read. He replied that he read very little; that he hardly found anything that was written from the heart and was really true. "Have you read Longfellow's Hyperion?" Sumner asked him. "Yes," he replied, "and I admire it very much; I think it a very great book." He then added in a very solemn manner, "I think I may say that Longfellow's 'Psalm of Life' saved me from suicide. I first found it on a scrap of newspaper, in the hands of two Irish women, soiled and worn; and I was at once touched by it."

The Chinese translator and noted scholar, Tung Tajen, a great admirer of Longfellow, sent the poet a Chinese fan, upon which was inscribed in Chinese characters a translation of the "Psalm of Life." The fan is one of the folding kind, and the characters are inscribed on it in vertical columns.

An Englishman serving on the staff of the American minister in China found this beautiful poem in Chinese and translated it back into English, not knowing that it had been written originally in English. Here is a verse of the translation he made. You will scarcely recognize the familiar—

> Tell me not, in mournful numbers,
> Life is but an empty dream!
> For the soul is dead that slumbers,
> And things are not what they seem.

AS TRANSLATED FROM THE CHINESE.

Do not manifest your discontent in a piece of verse:
A hundred years (of life) are, in truth, as one asleep (so soon are they gone);
The short dream (early death), the long dream (death after long life), alike are dreams (so little is the body concerned; after death)
There still remains the spirit (which is able to) fill the universe.

The words in parenthesis were not in the Chinese and the translator supplied them to complete the sense in English.

CHAPTER XI

HOW SOME OF THE GREAT POEMS WERE WRITTEN

We have already often spoken of the "Psalm of Life," perhaps the greatest poem Longfellow ever wrote. He composed it in his room at the Craigie House, which had been Washington's chamber. The death of his young wife had afflicted him deeply, and one day as he sat between two windows, looking sadly out, this poem came into his mind and he wrote it. For a long time no one knew of its existence, and it was not until many months later that he sent it to be published. "The Reaper and the Flowers" was written in much the same way, and "The Light of Stars" was composed on a serene and beautiful summer evening, exactly suggestive of the poem.

Longfellow himself tells how "The Wreck of the Hesperus" was written. Says he:

"This is one of the poems which I like to recall. It floats in my mind again and again, whenever I read of some of our frightful storms on the coast. Away back in the year when the 'Voices of the

Night' was published, in the closing month of the year, the New England coast was lashed by a terrible tempest: and there were numerous shipwrecks recorded. I remember reading in the newspapers one day of the loss of a schooner on the reef of Norman's Woe, called 'The Hesperus.' Norman's Woe is, as you are aware, a frowning mass of rocks, surrounded by the ocean, not far from Gloucester. It occurred to me to write a ballad, which I did some days afterwards, while I was sitting alone one night by the fire in the room above."

The fact is, after writing part of it he went to bed, and being unable to sleep, got up and wrote the remainder.

"Excelsior" probably stands next to the "Psalm of Life" as a popular favorite. One evening, also in that chamber of Washington's at the Craigie House, after he had been at a party, Longfellow caught sight of this word on a torn piece of newspaper. Lying near was a letter from Charles Sumner, and immediately he began to write on the back of this, crowding the stanzas in as best he could. Later he carefully rewrote the poem, and changed it in many parts. The next time Sumner visited the Craigie House he was shown the letter, and he asked to have it back. Longfellow gave it him, and Sumner always kept it as a treasure. When he died he left it by will to Harvard College.

Once in answer to a letter Longfellow gave the following explanation of the meaning of the poem:

"My intention in writing it was no more than to display, in a series of pictures, the life of a man of genius, resisting all temptations, laying aside all fears, heedless of all warnings, and pressing right on to accomplish his purpose. His motto is 'Excelsior'—higher. He passes through the Alpine village, through the rough, cold paths of the world, where the peasants cannot understand him, and where his watchword is 'an unknown tongue.' He disregards the happiness of domestic peace, and sees the glaciers—his fate—before him. He disregards the·warnings of the old man's wisdom and the fascinations of woman's love. He answers to all, 'Higher yet!' The monks of St. Bernard are

the representatives of religious forms and ceremonies; and with their oft-repeated prayer mingles
the sound of his voice, telling them there is something higher than forms or ceremonies. Filled
with these aspirations, he pushes forward; and the
voice heard in the air is the promise of immortality
and progress ever upward, without having reached
the perfection he longed for."

"The Village Blacksmith" is another poem with
a history. It will be remembered that we have
already said that Longfellow's great-grandfather
was a blacksmith. The "village smithy" "under
a spreading chestnut tree"—the one about which
Longfellow wrote the poem, though his grandfather
was never there—stood on Brattle Street, in Cambridge. After a time it had to be removed. Some
of the branches were cut off the chestnut tree,
that a dwelling-house might be put up, and it
then looked so ugly that the town authorities
ordered it to be cut down.

This made Longfellow feel very sad. The year
before he made a sketch of the shop and the tree,
just as they stood, and this rough sketch has been

published. On the morning the tree was cut down, every one crowded out to see the choppers at work, and gaze at the tree as it tumbled over.

On his seventy-second birthday the children of Cambridge presented Longfellow with an arm-chair made out of the wood of the old chestnut tree. It was a handsome chair, jet black and finely carved with horse chestnuts and leaves. Inscribed around it was a verse from the poem:

> And children coming home from school
>   Look in at the open door;
> They love to see the flaming forge,
>   And hear the bellows roar,
> And catch the burning sparks that fly
>   Like chaff from a threshing-floor.

The chair was upholstered in green leather, and there was a brass plate under the cushion, on which was inscribed:

" *To the author of ' The Village Blacksmith,' this chair, made from the wood of the spreading chestnut tree, is presented as an expression of grateful regard and veneration by the children of Cam-*

*bridge, who, with their friends, join in the best
wishes and congratulations on this anniversary,
Feb. 27, 1879."*

Longfellow was very much pleased by this and
wrote a poem to the children, entitled "From My
Arm-chair." You may read it in any volume of
his poems.

One more poem of which we must speak is
"The Skeleton in Armor." Said Longfellow once,
"This ballad was suggested to me while riding on
the seashore at Newport. A year or two previous
a skeleton had been dug up at Fall River, clad in
broken and corroded armor; and the idea occurred
to me of connecting it with the round tower at
Newport, generally known, hitherto, as the Old
Windmill, though now claimed by the Danes as
a work of their early ancestors."

When the poem was written some of Longfellow's friends, probably the members of that "Five
of Clubs," thought it was beneath his dignity; but
others were so enthusiastic about it that when one
of them read it aloud to him very appreciatively
he sprang to his feet and embraced him, and paid

no more attention to the criticisms. He was thinking about the subject, after his visit to the skeleton
that had been dug up, for more than a year before
the poem flashed into his mind.

CHAPTER XII

THE POET'S SECOND MARRIAGE

You will remember that at the time his first
wife died Longfellow was in Holland. For a long
time after that he kept very much secluded, and
in the "Footsteps of Angels" we have seen how
deeply the thought of his first wife was impressed
on his memory. But while he was traveling in
Switzerland the year after her death, he met Mr.
Nathan Appleton, a rich man of Boston who was
traveling with his family. His daughter Frances
Elizabeth was very beautiful and had many admir-
ers. Perhaps Longfellow fell in love with her then,
but if he did, it was doubtless because she seemed
very cold toward him.

When he got back to Cambridge and was settled in the Craigie House, he wrote a sort of novel entitled "Hyperion," which, like "Outre-Mer", described his journeyings in Europe, but which also had a romantic love story, in which most people thought that the hero, Paul Flemming, a young American man of letters, was Longfellow himself and the heroine, Mary Ashburton, was Miss Appleton. In the story, Mary Ashburton refused Paul Flemming's offer of marriage. It is not probable, however, that Longfellow said anything about love at that time; but when the novel was published and became popular it was whispered about that the young lady was very indignant.

Nevertheless, the Appletons and Longfellow had had a very pleasant time together in Europe. Once they stopped at the hotel called "The Raven." It was in the town of Zurich. First Mr. Appleton wrote his name in the register with some compliment to the house. Then the landlord presented a very long bill, which made Mr. Appleton angry and he was vexed because he had written something complimentary to the house.

"But I have not written my name," said Mr. Longfellow; "and, if you will allow me, I will treat the innkeeper as he deserves."

He took the register, and this is what he wrote in it:

Beware of the Raven of Zurich!
'Tis a bird of omen ill,
With a noisy and unclean nest,
And a very, very long bill.

Longfellow went home first, and for six or seven years lived, as we have seen, in Cambridge; but later he often visited Pittsfield, where the Appleton summer mansion was and where Miss Frances Elizabeth was staying, and there she finally consented to be his wife. They were married, and Mr. Appleton bought the Craigie House and presented it to them to keep house in.

Longfellow had five children, two sons and three daughters. When the Appletons lived at Lynn, one of the sons, Charles, was tipped over while in a sailboat and of course got soaking wet. In place of his shoes Mr. Appleton gave him a pair of old slippers. Longfellow returned them later with this parody of his own "Psalm of Life":

> Slippers that perhaps another,
>   Sailing o'er the Bay of Lynn,
> A forlorn or shipwrecked nephew,
>   Seeing, may purloin again.

His daughters, who became the comfort of his old age, are beautifully referred to in the poem called "The Children's Hour":

> I hear in the chamber above me
>   The patter of little feet,
> The sound of a door that is opened,
>   And voices soft and sweet.

> From my study I see in the lamp light,
>   Descending the broad hall stair,
> Grave Alice, and laughing Allegra,
>   And Edith with golden hair.

In 1861, twenty years before the poet himself died, Mrs. Longfellow was burned to death. She was sitting at her library table amusing her two youngest children by making seals. A bit of the burning wax fell on her light gauze dress, which was in a moment all aflame. She cried out, and

Longfellow came running from the next room and threw a rug about her; but she was so burned that she soon died, though several doctors came almost immediately. Longfellow himself was also frightfully burned, but not dangerously.

This, and the death of his other wife, were the two great sorrows of his life. Except for these two misfortunes, it would seem as though he were always fortunate, living, as it were, in a bed of roses—always successful, never poor, never discontented with his lot. But after the death of his second wife he was very gloomy for a long time.

It may be said that the sadness of the deaths of both wives made him write some of his best poems.

Three years after the death of Mrs. Longfellow, Hawthorne died.

Longfellow wrote a beautiful poem called "Hawthorne," which closes with this stanza:

Ah! who shall lift that wand of magic power,
   And the lost clew regain?
The unfinished window in Aladdin's tower,
   Unfinished must remain!

CHAPTER XIII

EVANGELINE, HIAWATHA, AND THE COURTSHIP
OF MILES STANDISH

After his first marriage we have seen that Long-fellow wrote his most famous short poems. After his second marriage he wrote his most famous long poems. The first was "Evangeline." It was published in 1847, four years after his marriage; but he had been a long time writing it. He once wrote, "I had the fever burning a long time in my brain before I let my hero take it. 'Evangeline' is so easy for you to read, because it was so hard for me to write."

The story of the Acadians is a familiar one. Acadia was the French name for Nova Scotia. But after the French had settled there the English claimed the land as having been discovered by John Cabot. There was much fighting between the French and English over the disputed ground, and finally the English made a settlement of their own at Halifax; but the country villages were made up mostly of the French. At last the rights of the English to the territory were acknowledged by the French government; but in the treaty that was made it was provided that the French settlers should not be obliged to pay taxes or take up arms against their fellow Frenchmen. Most of them also refused to take the customary oath of allegiance to the King of England.

To make up for the loss of this territory the French erected fortifications at Louisburg and Cape Breton, and they encouraged the Indians to keep up a raiding warfare on the English settlements. In this border warfare the English claimed that the French "neutrals" (as the Acadians were called) acted as spies and stirred up the Indians to revenge.

At last in 1755, a few years before the American Revolution, the colony of Massachusetts proposed an expedition against Acadia, and the British government fitted it out, They captured the neighboring French forts, and all the American people rejoiced at the easy victory. Then came the question, What should they do with those treacherous "neutrals," who were British subjects though they would not swear allegiance to Great Britain, and in heart and act remained loyal to France after France had been beaten off the ground.

"Scatter them through all the British colonies!" ordered the governor.

Accordingly, eighteen thousand of them were shipped off wherever it happened to be convenient to send them, and in such haste that families were separated, mothers and children parted, lovers torn from each other, and all thrown into a new world without money or property of any kind; for their houses and barns were burned, their crops destroyed, their money and goods confiscated. It was a horrible retribution for a very natural and simple-mined loyalty to their own native land and government.

A friend of Hawthorne's heard a story of a young couple who were about to be married on the day the proclamation was made; but as the young men were separated from their friends and families to prevent their taking up arms for their defense, the two were sent to different colonies, and spent the rest of their lives in a vain search for each other. At last they meet in a hospital, where the hero is dying. The story was offered to Hawthorne for a novel, but he did not care for it. One day when the friend, Hawthorne, and Longfellow were dining together, the story was told again to Longfellow and he was very much touched by it, especially by the constancy of the heroine.

"If you are not going to use it for a novel, give it to me for a poem," said Longfellow; and Hawthorne gladly consented.

The heroine of the poem was at first called Gabrielle; and the poet located the scene of the climax at a poorhouse in Philadelphia, with the charming surroundings of which he had been fascinated years before. While waiting for the sailing of the packet for Europe at the time of his first voyage, he wandered up Spruce street, where his attention was attracted to a large building with trees about it, inside of a high enclosure. He walked along to the great gate and stepped inside. The charming picture of a lawn, flower beds, and shade which it presented made an impression which never left him. When twenty-four years afterward he came to write "Evangeline," he located the final scene at this poorhouse, and the burial in an old Catholic graveyard not far away, which he had found by chance on another walk at the same period.

His next great poem was "Hiawatha." For ten years Longfellow had been thinking about writing an Indian poem. At last a young man who had been a pupil in one of his classes came back from the West, where he had been living among the Indians. One day while he was dining with the poet, he told many of his experiences among the red men. Longfellow was very much impressed, and looked about for a book where he might read old Indian legends. He found that a Mr. Schoolcraft had published such a book, entitled "Algic Researches." For three years, he says, he read and reread this volume. At last he began to write, and composed nearly five hundred lines, when he changed his mind and destroyed what he had written. He began again and continued writing to the end.

When "Hiawatha" was published, some critics claimed that it was stolen from a Finnish poem, and a great many people said unpleasant things about it. Already Poe had written very unkindly of "Evangeline," as he seemed to be jealous of Longfellow's success. But both "Evangeline" and "Hiawatha" soon became immensely popular, thousands of copies being sold and read.

Two years after "Hiawatha" appeared, the *Atlantic Monthly* was started. Longfellow, Holmes, Whittier, Emerson, Prescott and others, were called together at a dinner, and Lowell was chosen editor of the magazine. After the periodical was started and became so famous, the men who wrote for it met regularly once a month at a dinner. Longfellow was a contributor and an attendant at the dinners for a long time.

The year after the *Atlantic Monthly* was started, "The Courtship of Miles Standish" was published as a little volume. The poem professes to be a love poem, but the love is not so warm and sincere as that in the songs of Robert Burns.

CHAPTER XIV

THE GOOD OLD MAN

Longfellow was one of the best-natured men in the world. He was always pleasant and obliging to everybody who came to see him. He wrote his autograph for all the children who asked him. Once there was a school celebration in his honor. He was present and made a beautiful little speech, in which, among other things, he thanked the children of Cambridge for the arm-chair. When the exercises were over the children crowded about him and he wrote his name in their albums until he could write no more, his hand was so tired. But he told those who had not got his autograph that he would write it for them if they would come around to his house.

Many children went to see him on other occasions, and he was always very kind to them. Everybody loved him.

We have mentioned many of the men who were his friends. Another was Professor Agassiz, the great scientist and professor at Harvard College, who was a warm and intimate friend of Longfellow's.

After a time these friends began, one by one, to die. Agassiz died, Sumner died, and a number of others. Hawthorne had died some years before.

Longfellow lived a sad life after the terrible accident that killed his wife, and was getting to be a very old man. Every one tried to honor him. He knew that he was accounted the greatest poet America had produced. His sons and daughters were about him and took excellent care of him. Nevertheless, he began to weary of life a little, and longed to join the dear ones who had gone before.

> It is autumn; not without,
> But within me is the cold.
> Youth and spring are all about;
> It is I that have grown old.

He still wrote many beautiful poems, such as the "Tales of a Wayside Inn," "Keramos," and others. He even wrote a poem on the death of Garfield a short time before he himself died. But none of these poems became as famous as those he had written in earlier years in the prime of his manhood.

At last, on the 24th of March, 1882, he died, and the whole country went into mourning for him.

His soul to him who gave it rose;
God lead it to its long repose,
   Its glorious rest!
And though the poet's sun has set,
Its light shall linger round us yet,
   Bright, radiant, blest.

NOTE.—The thanks of the publishers are due Messrs. Houghton, Mifflin & Co. for their kind permission to use selections from the copyrighted works of Longfellow.

THE STORY OF

JOHN GREENLEAF WHITTIER

JOHN GREENLEAF WHITTIER

WHITTIER

CHAPTER I

THE QUAKER OF THE OLDEN TIME

The Quaker of the olden time!
How calm and firm and true,
Unspotted by its wrong and crime,
He walked the dark earth through!

The Quaker, with his broad-brimmed hat, his queer, old-fashioned coat, and his habit of saying "thee must" and "thee must not," was not only an honest man, but a good-natured, sensible man as well. The poet Whittier was a good Quaker, as "calm and firm and true" as the Quaker in his poem. He was also fond of children, and his best poems are about children and childhood days.

It is only a little over two hundred years since the first Quakers appeared. Whittier's great-great-grandfather, Thomas Whittier, was said to be a Huguenot by descent. He came from England, however, as a Puritan, and held various offices in the Puritan church in Salisbury and Haverhill, in northeastern Massachusetts, where he settled.

It happened that two Quakers, Joseph Peasley and Thomas Macy, who had come to Haverhill, were arrested and fined for "exhorting" on the Lord's day. They did it in their own houses; but in those Puritan times, all the exhorting had to be done in church by regular ministers. Thomas Whittier thought these men had been treated rather unjustly, and he and others petitioned the legislature, or General Court, to pardon them. But the old Puritans thought these petitioners about as bad as the "heretics" themselves, as the Quakers were regarded, and notified them that they must take back their petition or be punished. Thomas Whittier and Christopher Hussey, though not Quakers, refused, and were deprived of their right to vote; or, as it was called, "their rights as freemen."

Thomas Whittier was such a good, sensible man, however, that the people, although he was suspended from voting, had to ask him to help them do various things in the church; and after a while the General Court restored his "rights as a freeman." He himself never became a Quaker, but his son married a daughter of Joseph Peasley, and so most of the Whittiers after that were Quakers. Yet there were some who were not; for history tells of a Colonel Whittier about the time of the Revolution. He could not have been a Quaker, for no good Quaker ever goes into the army.

The Quakers are a peculiar people. They do not believe in fighting or going to war on any account. They are always for peace. The poet Whittier was opposed to war, and often wrote against it; and he refused to favor the Civil War, which freed the slaves, although he had himself been for many years a great anti-slavery reformer, along with his friend William Lloyd Garrison. But he admits that he had a sort of diabolical liking for the army and war, and once he wrote a war poem and had it published anonymously. He thought no one would ever know who wrote it, for it didn't sound much like a Quaker; but when he had become an old man some one did find it out, and he had to admit that he was its author.

Another thing the Quakers will not do is to swear, either in a profane way, or before a court of justice. They declare that the Scriptures say, "Swear not at all," and that it is just as wrong to swear in court as in anger. They are not great talkers; and in meeting, if no one has anything to say that is worth saying, they think it much better to sit in silence for an hour than to listen to a dull sermon.

Your grammars will tell you that it is just as incorrect to say "thee is," or "thee must," as it is to say "me is," or "him ought." It seems strange that most of the Quakers in the world, from the earliest time, should make a grammatical blunder like this. Of course Whittier, and many others, knew it was not correct; but they said that Quakers had used this form of speech from the very first, and they would not try to change the custom.

These queer people also said they were plain, sensible folk, and therefore would not cater to the "world and the devil" by wearing fine clothes. All dressed in the same way, in what was called

Quaker drab, the men with broad-brimmed beaver hats, the women with plain bonnets of black or "dove-colored" silk, unadorned with ribbons or other ornaments.

Neither did they have any music, nor indulge themselves in any unnecessary luxuries. They were sharp and shrewd, however, and as we shall see in the case of Whittier, did not forbear to have a little fun now and then.

The Puritans had revolted from the Church of England, and came to America for religious freedom. The Quakers had likewise revolted from the established forms of worship, but their belief was very different from that of the Puritans.

At first the Puritans in Massachusetts thought they would keep the Quakers out of their colony. They therefore punished severely every one who dared to come among them. They condemned four of them to death, and others they whipped and imprisoned and banished. But these persecutions did not prevent the Quakers from coming to Massachusetts, and finally the Puritans became ashamed of their intolerance, and left them to themselves.

CHAPTER II

A FARMER'S BOY

The first Thomas Whittier, after he married, built a log house, not far from the present Whittier homestead; but when he grew old and became well-to-do he put up what was then a fine house. This was as long ago as 1688, or thereabouts.

In this house, which is still standing, the poet John Greenleaf Whittier was born, December 17, 1807. His father was nearly fifty at the time of his birth, and twenty-one years older than his mother. His grandfather was about the same age when his father was born, and his great-grandfather and great-great-grandfather were equally old at the births of their sons.

On his mother's side Whittier was descended from a remarkable old preacher named Stephen Bachiler. This man had deep-set, bright eyes, and handsome features, which were inherited by most of his descendants, many of whom became famous men. One was Daniel Webster, who looked very much indeed like Whittier. Both had the Bachiler eye and brow.

New England farm life is not easy or pleasant, though Whittier never admitted that he didn't have a first-rate time when he was a boy, as you may see by reading "Snow-Bound." His father's family had to raise most of the food they ate. They had no comfortable sofas, and the chairs were very straight-backed. Besides, they did not succeed very well in keeping warm in the winter. As they thought it was necessary to toughen themselves, they went out on very cold days without much clothing on. Indeed, they probably had but very few warm clothes. There were no such things in those days as heavy flannels or great overcoats. The cloth in their garments was spun and woven at home by the mother, and she did not always get the threads very close together. So there were a great many spaces for the wind to blow through. Of course they had to go to meeting every First-day (Sunday), and as there were no fires in the meeting-house, they suffered much from the cold in winter.

Even the dwelling houses were not very warm. There was only one fire, and it was built in a chimney-place so large that there was room for benches inside the chimney next to the fire. Then the wind would come in through the cracks and crevices; and while it was very hot before the fire-place, a little way back it was cold. It would often happen on cold, windy nights that their faces would burn while their backs were almost freezing. And the bedrooms were like ice-chests, and never warm except in summer, when they were sure to be too hot. Whittier was sickly all the latter part of his life; and he laid his trouble largely to exposure in childhood; for he was always delicate. He lived to be very old, however, as did all his ancestors.

This was the unpleasant side to his boyhood; of the pleasant side Whittier himself has told us. If you wish to know what good times he had in the summer season, read the "Barefoot Boy":

> Blessings on thee, little man,
> Barefoot boy with cheeks of tan! . . .
> From my heart I give thee joy—
> I was once a barefoot boy!

It is only the country boy who knows—

> How the tortoise bears his shell,
> How the woodchuck digs his cell,
> And the ground-mole sinks his well;
> How the robin feeds her young,
> How the oriole's nest is hung;
> Where the whitest lilies blow,
> Where the freshest berries grow,
> Where the groundnut trails its vine,
> Where the wood-grape's clusters shine.

But it is in "Snow-Bound," his greatest and most beautiful poem, that we hear of all the pleasant times which the farm boy has in winter, and also all about the members of Whittier's own family. He begins the poem by telling how the snowstorm came up, and then goes on—

> Meanwhile we did our nightly chores,—
> Brought in the wood from out of doors,
> Littered the stalls, and from the mows
> Raked down the herd's-grass for the cows.

Every farmer boy knows what "chores" are. The fun came the next morning when their father, "a prompt, decisive man," wasting no breath, said, "Boys, a path!" You must go to the poem itself to read about the Aladdin's cave they dug in the snow, and the other things they did. "As night drew on," says the poet,

We piled with care our nightly stack
Of wood against the chimney back,—
The oaken log, green, huge and thick
And on its top the stout back stick;
The knotty forestick laid apart,
And filled between with curious art
The ragged brush; then, hovering near,
We watched the first red blaze appear,
Heard the sharp crackle, caught the gleam
On whitewashed wall and sagging beam,
Until the old, rude-furnished room,
Burst flower-like into rosy bloom. . . .
Shut in from all the world without,
We sat the clean-winged hearth about.
Content to let the north wind roar
In baffled rage at pane and door;
While the red logs before us beat
The frost line back with tropic heat;
And ever, when a louder blast
Shook beam and rafter as it passed,

The merrier up its roaring draught
The great throat of the chimney laughed.
The house dog on his paws outspread
Laid to the fire his drowsy head,
The cat's dark silhouette on the wall
A couchant tiger's seemed to fall;
And, for the winter fireside meet,
Between the andirons' straddling feet,
The mug of cider simmered slow,
The apples sputtered in a row,
And, close at hand, the basket stood
With nuts from brown October's wood

Whittier was nearly sixty years old when he wrote this poem, and perhaps he had forgotten partly the hardships of his boyhood; but the poem is so great because it is so simple and natural and true. It may seem strange that the greatest work of a great poet is no more than a description of his every-day home when he was a boy. Whittier's home was not finer nor better than anybody else's home—than yours or mine; in fact, in comparison with what we have, it was very poor indeed. Yet Whittier made this wonderful poem about it. That shows how great a poet he was. Only a great

poet could take a barefoot boy, or a snowstorm, or
a common farmhouse and write such beautiful
verses about it. Think of this carefully, and you
will come to understand what good poetry really is.

CHAPTER III

WHITTIER'S FAMILY

Most people are blessed with brothers and sisters,
with whom they grow up. First one and then the
other is sent away to school. Soon they are all out
in the world, earning livings for themselves; they
get married and have families of their own; and
before long they seem to forget the home of their
childhood But Whittier did not get married, and
one of his sisters did not marry. He lived on the
farm most of the time till he was thirty years
old, when he moved with his mother and sister to
Amesbury. We are therefore more than usually
interested in knowing about the members of the
family in which he was born.

First, there was his father. He was a plain,

matter-of-fact man, and did not believe in poetry; and so, in this, young Greenleaf received very little encouragement from him.

The encouragement in his poetic efforts, which the father failed to give, he got from his mother, sisters, and brother, who were all proud of him. His mother was a dear, sweet Quaker lady, as saintly as she was lovely. Her face was full and fair, and she had fine, dark eyes. She appreciated poetry and all fine and delicate sentiments, and for fifty years she was the guide, counselor, and friend of her illustrious son.

Greenleaf had a brother, Matthew Franklin, several years younger than himself, who outlived every one else in the family except the poet. He had also two sisters, the eldest of the family, and the youngest. The elder sister, Mary, married and lived in Haverhill; but the younger never married, and was the poet's intimate friend and housekeeper until both were old. In "Snow-Bound" the reader will find this beautiful description of her, lines as sweet and beautiful as the poet ever wrote:

Upon the motley-braided mat
Our youngest and our dearest sat,
Lifting her large, sweet, asking eyes,
  Now bathed within the fadeless green
And holy peace of Paradise. . . .
I tread the pleasant paths we trod,
I see the violet-sprinkled sod
Whereon she leaned, too frail and weak
The hillside flowers she loved to seek,
Yet following me where'er I went
With dark eyes full of love's content.

    .   .   .   .   .

And yet, dear heart! remembering thee,
  Am I not richer than of old?
Safe in thy immortality,
  What change can reach the wealth I hold?
  What chance can mar the pearl and gold
Thy love hath left in trust with me ?—
And when the sunset gates unbar,
  Shall I not see thee waiting stand,
And, white against the evening star,
  The welcome of thy beckoning hand?

The poem ''Snow-Bound'' was written perhaps
as a memorial of her. He and she had been for
fifty years as loving and fond as husband and

wife, but held together by a purer, more spiritual bond.

She was a poet like her brother; and to this day, in any complete edition of Whittier's poems you will find, towards the end of the volume, "Poems by Elizabeth H. Whittier," which he wished to be always printed with his.

In this family there were two other kindly souls. One was Uncle Moses, a brother of the poet's father, "innocent of books, but rich in lore of fields and brooks." The other was Aunt Mercy, Mrs. Whittier's sister:—

> The sweetest woman ever Fate
> Perverse denied a household mate,
> Who, lonely, homeless, not the less
> Found peace in love's unselfishness,
> And welcome wheresoe'er she went.

Such was the Whittier family, all good Quakers, dressing in Quaker fashion, and talking in the quaint Quaker way; but they were all cheerful and ready for enjoyment, and all were fond and devoted and gentle and ambitious to live well.

CHAPTER IV

STORIES OF THE POET'S CHILDHOOD

The Whittiers seem to have been a simple-minded family. Some stories told of the poet in his childhood would almost make you think him stupid, but no one seems ever to interpret them in that way.

He remembered nothing that happened before he was six years old; but about that time he heard that a neighboring farm had been sold at auction. The next morning he went out and was surprised to find the land still there, instead of a big hole in the ground; for he seemed to think that after the farm was sold it would be taken away.

When he was nine years old, President Monroe visited Haverhill, and happened to be there on the same day that a menagerie came to town. The Quaker boy was not allowed to see either. He thought he did not care much for the wild beasts, but he would have liked to see the greatest man in the United States. The next day he trudged over to the village, hoping to see at least some foot-prints that the great man had left behind him. He found at last the impressions of an elephant's feet in the road, and supposing these to be the tracks of the President, he followed them as far as he could make them out. Then he went home satisfied that he had seen the footsteps of the greatest man in the country.

At another time he and his brother calculated that if each could lift the other by his boot straps, first one lifting and then the other, they might lift themselves up to the ceiling, and no telling how much higher. Of course when they tried it they didn't get very far.

In later life he used to tell a story of how children sometimes suffer needlessly, and in ways of which their parents little dream. When he went to ride with his father, they used to walk up a certain hill, in order to rest the horse. By the side of the road there was a gander, which had come out from a neighboring farmyard; and he says he would rather in later life have walked up to a hostile can-non than as a child go by that gander. But he was ashamed to let his father know his fear, and so walked past in an agony of dread.

There is also told an interesting story of an ox named Old Butler. One day Greenleaf went out with some salt for the oxen. He was climbing up the side of a steep hill when Old Butler, on top, saw him, and came plunging down. The hill was so steep that the ox could not stop, and in a moment he would have crushed the young master; but gathering himself together at the right moment, the creature by a great effort leaped straight out into the air over the head of the boy. It was the wonderful intelligence of this ox that saved young Greenleaf's life.

Another amusing story is also told of this ox. Once a Quaker meeting was being held in the kitchen. Unexpectedly the ox stuck his head in at the window. While a sweet-voiced sister was speaking he listened quietly; but when a loud-voiced brother began to speak, he drew out his head, flung up his tail, and went off bellowing. This the children thought very funny and a good joke on the brother.

CHAPTER V

SCHOOL DAYS

Brisk wielder of the birch and rule,
The master of the district school
Held at the fire his favored place.
Its warm glow lit a laughing face,
Fresh-hued and fair, where scarce appeared
The uncertain prophecy of beard.
He teased the mitten-blinded cat,
Played cross-pins on my uncle's hat,
Sang songs, and told us what befalls
In classic Dartmouth's college halls.

　　.　　.　　.　　.　　.　　.

A careless boy that night he seemed;
　But at his desk he had the look
And air of one who wisely schemed,
　And hostage from the future took
　In trained thought and lore of book.
Large-brained, clear-eyed—of such as he
Shall Freedom's young apostles be.

　　　　　　　　—Snow-Bound.

Until he was nineteen Whittier went only to the

district school, and he used to say that in all that time only two of the teachers were worth anything at all. Both of these were Dartmouth students, and are fairly well described in the above quotation from "Snow-Bound." One was Joshua Coffin, Whittier's first teacher. He came back again some years later, and often spent his evenings at the Whittier homestead. In later years he was the poet's friend and helper in the antislavery cause.

Little Greenleaf started to school when he was very small, and before he had learned his letters. Among his poems is a sweet little one, entitled "In School Days." He begins by describing the schoolhouse:

> Within, the master's desk is seen,
> Deep scarred by raps official;
> The warping floor, the battered seats,
> The jack-knife's carved initial.

You must read for yourself the story of the little boy and the little girl, and how the latter said:

" I 'm sorry that I spelt the word:
I hate to go above you,
Because," —the brown eyes lower fell,—
" Because, you see, I love you!"

Of books to read they had not many in the Whittier household, and most of them were the works of saintly Quakers. The Bible was the chief book, and that they read until they had it by heart. Joshua Coffin used to bring various books which he had and read them aloud to the older people, not paying much attention to the boy of fifteen who sat in the corner and listened. Once he brought a volume of Burns's poems and read page after page, explaining the Scotch dialect. Greenleaf, then a tall, shy lad, listened spellbound. He had got into what his Uncle Moses called his "stood." The teacher saw that he was interested, and offered to leave the book with him. That was about the first good poetry he had ever heard. It kindled the fire of poetic genius in his own mind and heart, and he soon began to write poetry himself. But he was only a farmer's lad, and writing

poetry does not come easy to one in such surroundings.

While he was in his teens he made his first visit
to Boston, staying with a relative who was post-
master of the city. You may imagine how he
looked, a gawky country boy, with broad-brimmed
Quaker hat and plain, homespun clothes. But he
wore for the first time in his life "boughten buttons" on his coat, and his Quaker hat had been
covered by his Aunt Mercy with drab velvet.
These made him feel very fine.

He was induced to buy a copy of Shakespeare;
and at the table of his relative was a brilliant lady,
who was very kind to him. He had been warned
against the temptations of the town, and you can
imagine how shocked he was to find out that this
fine lady was an actress. She invited him to go to
the theater; but he hastily declined, and was
almost ashamed of himself for having bought a
volume of plays, even if they were Shakespeare's.

Somehow or other a copy of one of the Waverley
novels came into the Quaker home, and Whittier
and his sister read it together without letting their

parents know. They read late into the night; and at one time, just as they were getting to an exciting part, the candle burned out and they had to go to bed in the dark, for it was quite impossible to get another.

There is a story that Whittier's first verses were written on the beam of his mother's loom. At any rate he wrote verses on his slate in school, and passed them around among the scholars. One stanza his sister remembered, and repeated afterward:

> And must I always swing the flail,
> And help to fill the milking-pail?
> I wish to go away to school;
> I do not wish to be a fool.

The desk on which the poet wrote his first verses was built by that original Thomas Whittier, more than a hundred years before Greenleaf was born. It stood in the kitchen for many years; then it was packed away. But a few years before Whittier died, a niece of his had it taken out and repaired, and he used it until the end of his life.

In those old days his sister Mary thought his verses exceedingly fine, quite as good as those she read in the "Poet's Corner" of the *Free Press.* This paper had just been started in Newburyport by William Lloyd Garrison, who was only three years older than Whittier, but had had every advantage of education. John Whittier, the father, liked the solid tone of it, and subscribed. Without letting her brother know, Mary got one of his poems and sent it anonymously to the editor of the paper. When, a week or so afterward, the postman came along by the field where the Whittiers were at work and flung the paper over the fence, Greenleaf looked at once to see what was in the "Poet's Corner," and was immensely surprised to see his own poem there. He says he simply stood and stared at it, without reading a word. His father suggested that he had better go to work; but he couldn't help opening the paper again and looking at his own poem.

Another poem was sent, and Garrison wrote a note to introduce it, in which he said: "His poetry bears the stamp of true poetic genius, which, if carefully cultivated, will rank him among the bards of his country." How strange a prophecy, and how strange the fortune that brought together the great reformer, William Lloyd Garrison, and the great poet, John Greenleaf Whittier, when both were so young and inexperienced!

CHAPTER VI

HAVERHILL ACADEMY

It was a happy day for Whittier when his sister sent that stolen poem to the paper edited by William Lloyd Garrison, for Garrison immediately took a fancy to the author. After printing the second poem sent, he learned from what part of Haverhill the poems came, and drove out fourteen miles to see the young author.

He was a neatly dressed, handsome, and affable young gentleman, and came with a lady friend. As it was a hot summer day, Whittier was at work in the fields, wearing doubtless little beside an old straw hat, a shirt, and a pair of overalls. His bashfulness made him wish to avoid seeing the fine city visitor; but his sister persuaded him. He slipped in at the back door and changed his clothes, and a long and interesting visit with Garrison followed. They became fast friends, and in later years were workers together in the cause of the slave.

Friend Whittier, the old gentleman, came into the room while the two were having their first talk, and Garrison told him he ought to send his son away to school. The old gentleman was not at all pleased by the turn affairs were taking, and told young Garrison that he ought not to put such notions into the boy's head. As we have already said, Friend Whittier, being a matter-of-fact Quaker, did not approve of poetry anyway.

So this time passed by, and Greenleaf was kept at work on the farm. Garrison gave up his paper in Newburyport and went to Boston, and the young poet sent his verses to the *Haverhill Gazette*. A Mr. Thayer was the editor of this paper, and he conceived the same opinion of the lad that Garrison had. He also went to the old gentleman and urged him to give his son a classical education. An academy was to be opened in Haverhill that fall, and young Whittier could attend it and spend part of each week at home. Two years before, Greenleaf had seriously injured himself by undertaking some very hard work on the farm; indeed from this strain he suffered all his life. On account of this, his father considered the matter more favorably.

Mr. Thayer, the editor, promised to board the young man in his family; but it was a serious question as to where the small amount of money needed was to come from. There was a mortgage of $600 on the farm, and nearly all the ready money that could be obtained went to pay taxes and interest on the debt. The young man received permission to attend the academy; but he must pay his own way.

It was not an easy thing to pick up spare change in those days, as the elder Whittier well knew; but Greenleaf looked cheerfully about. An opportunity soon appeared. A hired man on his father's farm occupied his winters in making a kind of cheap slippers, which he sold for twenty-five cents a pair. He promised to teach the young poet the art of making them. It was not hard to learn. During the winter of 1826–27 he made enough to keep him at the academy six months. He calculated so closely that he thought he would have twenty-five cents more than enough to pay his expenses of board, books, and clothes. At the end of the term, sure enough, he had that twenty-five cents left.

James F. Otis, a noted lawyer, read some of Whittier's poems, and, like Garrison, determined to go and find him. He was told that he was a shoemaker in Haverhill. He says that he found him at work in his shoe shop, and making himself known to him, they spent the day together in wandering over the hills, and on the shores of the Merrimac River, talking about matters literary. Like Garrison, Otis later became an intimate friend of Whittier.

When the Haverhill academy was opened, Whittier was not only to become a pupil; but he contributed the ode that was sung. This gave him a sort of social send-off in the town, and henceforth he was something of a personage in Haverhill. In the year 1827 he contributed forty-seven poems to the *Haverhill Gazette* alone, and forty-nine in 1828.

So the young poet that William Lloyd Garrison discovered and went fourteen miles to see was beginning to become famous.

CHAPTER VII

THE FRIENDSHIP OF GOOD WOMEN

If Whittier ever had a real love affair, no one seems to have known about it. The fact is, he was not of the passionate kind. But all his life his best friends were women, and many a good woman he knew and was fond of, and he and she became real friends. And of that friendship with him, all those women, without exception, were proud indeed. In a letter written a dozen years after his school life began, he says:

"For myself, I owe much to the kind encouragement of female friends. A bashful, ignorant boy, I was favored by the kindness of a lady who saw, or thought she saw, beneath the clownish exterior something which gave promise of intellect and worth. [This was the wife of Mr. Thayer, with whom he boarded.] The powers of my own mind, the mysteries of my own spirit, were revealed to myself, only as they were called out by one of those dangerous relations called cousins, who, with all her boarding school glories upon her, condescended to smile upon my rustic simplicity. She was so learned in the, to me, more than occult mysteries of verbs and nouns, and philosophy, and botany, and mineralogy, and French, and all that, and then she had seen something of society, and could talk (an accomplishment at that time to which I could lay no claim), that on the whole I looked upon her as a being to obtain whose good opinion no effort could be too great."

One of these young lady friends, perhaps the very cousin of whom he speaks, wrote of him years afterwards:

"He was nearly nineteen when I first saw him. He was a very handsome, distinguished-looking young man. His eyes were remarkably beautiful. He was tall, slight, and very erect; a bashful youth, but never awkward, my mother said, who was a better judge of such matters than I. . . .

"With intimate friends he talked a great deal, and in a wonderfully interesting manner; usually earnest, and frequently playful. He had a great deal of wit. It was a family characteristic. . . . The influence of his Quaker bringing-up was manifest. I think it was always his endeavor

to render less
The sum of human wretchedness.

This, I say, was his steadfast endeavor, in spite of his inborn love of teasing. He was very modest, never conceited, never egotistic. One could never flatter him. I never tried, but I have seen people attempt it, and it was a signal failure. He did not flatter, but told some very wholesome and unpalatable truths."

An amusing story is told of Whittier's love of teasing. At the time it happened he must have been between thirty and forty. A Quaker sister named Sophronia Page, who went about preaching to little gatherings of the Friends, stopped one night at his mother's house. As most Quaker bonnets are precisely alike, there is no way of telling them apart except by the name inside. When Sophronia Page went away she put on Mrs. Whittier's bonnet by mistake. When she got to the next stopping place and saw the name inside, she sent the bonnet back. Whittier noticed it in a box in the hall, and thought he would have some fun with his mother.

"What does thee think Sophronia Page has done?" he asked her, sitting down.

"I don't know, Greenleaf," she said quietly. "What is it?"

"Something I'm much afraid she will be called up in Yearly Meeting for."

"I hope she hasn't been meddling with the troubles of the Friends," said Mrs. Whittier, anxiously, referring to some church quarrels.

"Worse than that!" said the young man, while his mother got more and more excited. "She has been taking other people's things, and has just begun to send some of them back."

With that he went into the hall and brought back the bonnet.

"If thee were twenty years younger I would take thee over my knee!" said his mother when she saw what it was all about.

Among his other famous women friends was Mrs. Sigourney, the poetess, with whom he became acquainted in Hartford while he was editing a paper there. He also knew Lucy Larcom; and it was said at one time that he was engaged to marry Lucy Hooper, but there was no truth in this. Her death, shortly afterwards, made him feel very sad. In his poetic works you may find poems addressed to both these women.

While speaking of women we must not omit a description of that woman who was to him dearest of all women in the world, his sister Lizzie. This gifted sister Lizzie was "the pet and pride of the household, one of the rarest women, her brother's complement, possessing all the readiness of speech and facility of intercourse which he wanted; taking easily in his presence the lead in conversation, which the poet so gladly abandoned to her, while he sat rubbing his hands and laughing at her daring sallies. She was as unlike him in person as

in mind; for his dignified erectness, she had end-
less motion and vivacity; for his regular and handsome features, she had a long Jewish nose, so full
of expression that it seemed to enhance, instead of
injuring, the effect of the large and liquid eyes that
glowed with merriment and sympathy behind it.
. . . Her quick thoughts came like javelins; a saucy
triumph gleamed in her great eyes; the head moved
a little from side to side with the quiver of a weapon,
and lo! you were transfixed."

During his long life this sister was to Whittier
more than sweetheart or wife, for she had the wit
and the sympathy of all womankind in her one
frail form; and Whittier knew it and depended on
it for his happiness.

CHAPTER VIII

POLITICAL AMBITION

Young Whittier remained at Haverhill academy
only two terms. We have seen that he paid for
the first one by making shoes. The second he paid
for by teaching school. When he went to the

committee to be examined for this school he felt rather nervous; but the committee asked him only for a specimen of his handwriting, which was very neat and clear.

He decided not to go to college, because he said he wouldn't live on the charities of others, and it would have been impossible to get through college without borrowing money of friends. Poor as he was, Whittier never borrowed money.

While in Haverhill he wrote a great many poems and articles for the local newspaper. Garrison was then in Boston editing a temperance paper. But soon he thought he had something better in view, and concluded to turn the editorship over to Whittier. Whittier accepted the position and went to Boston; but he was to edit the *Manufacturer*, not the *Philanthropist*. Both were published by the same people. This is the way he writes about his work:

"The *Manufacturer* goes down well, thanks to the gullibility of the public, and we are doing well, very well. Have had one or two rubs from other papers, but I have had some compliments which were quite as much as my vanity could swallow. Have tolerable good society, Mrs. Hale and her literary club, etc. I am coming out for the tariff by and by—have done something at it already— but the *astonisher* is yet to come! Shall blow Cambreling and McDuffie sky-high."

Cambreling and McDuffie were politicians whom he was going to oppose.

We should hardly think that the gentle poet Whittier, Quaker as he was, would conceive the ambition to become a politician; but he was editing a political newspaper, and soon got deep into politics and liked it.

He had not been in Boston long when, his father becoming ill, he went back to the farm and remained there until the old gentleman died, in June, 1830. He spent all his time in study and writing, however, and after his father's death he was asked to edit a political paper in Hartford, Connecticut. He didn't know anything about Connecticut politics; but he took hold and soon learned how matters stood. Everybody liked him and he made some excellent friends there.

Of course rival political newspapers are always saying sharp things about one another. After he had been in Hartford a few weeks he opened a copy of the *Catskill Recorder* and saw a long article headed ''John G. Whittier,'' in which he was abused and ridiculed unmercifully. He hid the paper so that no one should see it, and went around in fear and trembling, thinking every one would know about it. Finally he wrote to the editor of the paper, protesting; but the editor had another paragraph, saying that, if he was as ''thin-skinned'' as that, he had better keep out of politics. Soon after this the New York papers, among them Bryant's *Evening Post*, spoke of him and his editorship in a very complimentary manner, and he felt better.

The fact is, Whittier was a good politician. He managed affairs in Haverhill for years, and had a sort of party of his own which controlled things. Once on election day a tipsy man asked for a ride with him into town, and said that if Whittier would give him the ride he would vote for his candidate. Usually the man had voted on the other side.

Whittier said, "All right," and took him along. He supported the man to the polls, put the right ballot in his hand, and told him to vote. But the fellow was so intoxicated he was obstinate, and determined to vote the other way. At the last moment somebody handed him the wrong ballot, and he put it in the box.

There was in Haverhill district a politician who did not really belong to Whittier's party, but who had always been elected after giving written pledges. After he had been elected in this way for several terms, and had been forced by Whittier to live up to his promises, he determined to go in without pledges. Whittier was away, and so he wrote a noncommittal letter, referring to his past record, and saying he didn't intend to pledge himself any further. But Whittier came back in the nick of time, saw the danger, and went over to see the man, whose name was Caleb Cushing. Whittier told him he would not be elected unless he signed the desired pledges. After a while he said he would sign anything Whittier wrote. So the young politician sat down and wrote a letter, which

Mr. Cushing copied and signed. It was printed as a circular and sent all around town, and Cushing was elected. Then after he was elected Whittier watched him closely, and saw that he made good the promises in that letter. Some time after, he was on the point of being made a cabinet officer by the party to which Whittier was opposed; but by the use of this letter Whittier prevented it.

CHAPTER IX

THE GREAT QUESTION OF SLAVERY

It is altogether probable that Whittier would have been elected to Congress, and have had perhaps a great political career, had it not been for an act of genuine sacrifice on his part, made for the sake of right and conscience.

In 1833 Garrison pointed out to him that the country must be roused on the question of slavery. As a good Quaker, Whittier was already an abolitionist. He felt deeply the insufferable wrong that American citizens, even though black, should be slaves under the whip of a master. In an early poem he cries passionately:

What, ho!—our countryman in chains!
  The whip on woman's shrinking flesh!
Our soil yet reddening with the stains
  Caught from her scourging warm and fresh!
What! mothers from their children riven!
  What! God's own image bought and sold!
Americans to market driven,
  And bartered as the brute for gold!

When Garrison's appeal came, Whittier was at home on the farm, having given up the editorship of the Hartford paper on account of illness. Caleb Cushing, seven years younger than he, had come home from Europe and through Whittier's influence had been elected to Congress. Whittier's own name was being mentioned. A life of political ambition seemed to lie open before him. But with Garrison's appeal, he began a thorough and careful investigation of the question of slavery and its abolition in the United States. At last he wrote a pamphlet entitled "Justice and Expediency." It was a brilliant defense of the antislavery position. This he had published at his own expense, poor as he was. When it was about ready to appear he hesitated, and considered the situation carefully. The abolitionists were a poor, despised party. If he cast in his lot with them, none of the great political parties would have anything to do with him: he must give up his political ambition, and devote himself to a cause that would require years for its success, even if it should ever succeed.

In after times a boy of fifteen, who was ambitious in a political way, came to him for advice. Whittier said that as a young man his ideal had been the life of a prominent politician. From this he had been persuaded only by the appeals of his friends—chiefly Garrison. Taking their advice, he had united with the persecuted and obscure band of abolitionists, and to this course he attributed all his after success in life. Then, turning to the boy, he placed his hand on his head, and said in his gentle voice: "My lad, if thou wouldst win success, join thyself to some unpopular but noble cause."

From this time on, for thirty years, Whittier continued to be a very poor man. He made anti-slavery speeches sometimes, edited antislavery papers, wrote antislavery poems, was secretary of antislavery societies. For all this he was paid very little, and at the same time his health was poor. He sold the farm which had been his father's, and moved to Amesbury, where he lived for the remainder of his life.

His mother and his sister approved of his course, and supported him in every way. Their enthusiastic help made his life even pleasant. He thought nothing of poverty or hardship, but only of the great work into which he had thrown himself. At one time he thought he must mortgage his home; but a friend came to his assistance, and at last in his old age he had money and comfort and all that success brings with it.

From this time on, Whittier went through times of terrible struggle and conflict. Garrison had started his well-known paper, the *Liberator*, in Boston. To it Whittier contributed the poem from which we have quoted the verse on page 44. In 1835 he was elected to the legislature by his fellow townsmen of Haverhill.

While attending a special session of the legislature that year, he saw the mob which came near hanging Garrison, and saw the rope about his friend's neck as the crowd hurried him around the corner of a street. The riot started in an attempt to break up a meeting of the Female Antislavery Society, which Whittier's sister was attending. When he heard of the outbreak he hurried off to the rescue of his sister; but she and the other women had escaped; and the police finally saved Garrison and took him to the jail for protection.

CHAPTER X

HOW WHITTIER WAS MOBBED

We must now mention a few exciting events in which Whittier himself took part. At the time of the occurrences referred to in the last chapter, George Thompson, an eloquent English reformer

who had helped to secure the abolition of slavery
in the British colonies, came to Boston to speak
against slavery in the United States. It happened that the good people of the churches
thought that the easy way to remove slavery was
to send the slaves back to Africa, and for this they
took up collections. Garrison and Whittier came
out strongly against this weak-kneed plan, and
George Thompson helped them. Of course, the
church folk were angry; and all the business men
were angry, because they said it spoiled business
to stir up this agitation. As a result, the rough
characters in every town saw a chance to have
sport, and did all they could to break up the
meetings of abolitionists. The good church people and all the well-to-do and solid members of
the community were so angry that they wouldn't
do anything to stop the mobs; and the result was
that, wherever the speakers went, stones and rotten
eggs were thrown at them, and abuse of all sorts
was heaped upon them.

They got up a cry against George Thompson
especially, that he was an Englishman who had

come over to try to steal American business; for in those days Americans were very jealous of England. They said Thompson's antislavery speeches were intended simply to stir up a quarrel between the Northern people and the Southern, so that England could step in and get their business. Handbills were thrown broadcast in Boston offering one hundred dollars to the first person that would lay violent hands on him.

The first mob was the one Whittier saw in Boston, from which his sister narrowly escaped. The rioters were after Thompson; but not finding him, they took Garrison instead.

A little later Thompson came to Haverhill and stopped with the Whittiers. He and the poet immediately set out on a tour into New Hampshire. With Thompson had come a clergyman named Samuel J. May. He was to have held a meeting one Sunday in the First Parish meeting-house in Concord, but the committee refused to allow him to speak on slavery, and another church was obtained.

At half-past seven he began to speak. Every

one was listening with breathless attention, when a stone came through a window. He paid no attention, but kept steadily on. In a moment another stone came through the pulpit window, and another big one fell among the audience and frightened them so they all started for the door. Rev. Mr. May then decided to close the meeting, and called to the people to receive the benediction.

It was a good` thing he did so, for the steps of the church had been taken away, and if the crowd had poured out they would have fallen headlong. A heavily loaded cannon had also been brought up, and would have been used with terrible effect had the meeting lasted much longer. Whittier's sister took one arm of the clergyman, and another young lady the other, and they got him through the crowd without injury.

Whittier and Thompson had in the meantime gone to meet a still more violent mob. A man named George Kent arranged a meeting for them in Concord, Massachusetts, since famous as the home of Hawthorne and Emerson. Handbills were circulated announcing that George Thompson and John G. Whittier would hold a meeting "at which the principles, views, and operations of the abolitionists would be explained." The selectmen warned the people who were promoting it that there would be trouble if they held it; but they persisted.

As the hour for the meeting approached, a great crowd gathered. The selectmen ordered that the doors should not be opened. Thereupon the crowd determined that they would find "the incendiary George Thompson," and punish him as he deserved; and, with loud threats, they accordingly set off for the house of George Kent and his "wine cellar."

On the way they met Whittier. They thought he was Thompson, in spite of his Quaker coat and the assurances of a gentleman who was with him that he was not the man, and began to pelt him with rotten eggs, mud, and stones. Whittier was only lamed a little; but his coat was spoiled by the decayed eggs so that he could not wear it any more. Years afterward, when clothes were being sent to the negroes in the South, he donated this coat.

At last Whittier and his companion escaped into the house of Colonel Kent, a brother of George Kent, and the colonel convinced the crowd that Thompson was not there. They therefore pushed on to the house of George Kent, where he really was. Quite a little company of anti-slavery people had assembled there to see Thompson, among them two nieces of Daniel Webster. But when the crowd arrived, he had left the house by a back street.

When the mob found that he was gone, they went away to celebrate with fireworks and bon-fires. In the meantime Whittier, anxious for his friend, changed his hat, and escaping through the crowd went to the house of George Kent. After a time Thompson came back. So did the crowd, all the time firing guns, throwing stones, and making a great noise.

At last, early in the morning, a horse and buggy were brought around to the back door, and Thompson and Whittier got into the vehicle.

Then the gates were thrown open, and, before the crowd knew what was being done, they drove away at a furious rate and escaped.

They drove fast; but the news had spread before them. They came to an inn at some distance from Concord. A number of men were telling about the riot, and exhibiting a handbill calling upon all good citizens to assist in capturing George Thompson and giving him his deserts.

"How will you recognize the rascal?" asked Whittier.

"Easily enough; he is a tonguey fellow," said the landlord.

When they were in their carriage ready to drive away, Whittier said, "I am John G. Whittier, and this is George Thompson."

The men stared at them until they were out of sight, but did not offer to lay hands on them.

A year or two later Whittier went to Philadelphia to edit an antislavery paper. The abolitionists had put up a large, fine building, called Pennsylvania Hall. Whittier moved his editorial office into it as soon as it was finished. A series of

meetings were at once held in it; but they did not
last long, for one night a mob burned the building, and of course Whittier's office, with all his
papers, was destroyed.

CHAPTER XI

SOME OF WHITTIER'S FAMOUS POEMS

It is not necessary to tell all the events of those
years of struggle and hardship and poverty.
Whittier wrote a great many poems on slavery. A
volume containing one hundred of them was published without his knowledge in 1837 by Isaac
Knapp, publisher of the *Liberator* in Boston. It
was entitled ''Poems Written during the Progress
of the Abolition Question in the United States,
between the years 1830 and 1838. By John G.
Whittier.'' He was in New York when it
came out. It was the first edition of his poems
ever published. The next year he edited a volume
of antislavery poems entitled ''The North Star,''
only a few of which he contributed. In 1839 the

financial agent of the antislavery society, Joseph Healy, published a volume of poems by Whittier. There were 180 pages in the book, half of which was devoted to poems on slavery, the remainder to miscellaneous poems.

So the years passed by, and Whittier and his friends kept up the great fight against slavery. The poet wrote hundreds of pieces, poetry and prose, which were published in all sorts of papers all over the country. Now he was at Haverhill in politics, always working for the cause of the slave, now in Philadelphia or somewhere else editing a paper; and again at his home in Amesbury recovering his health.

In the meantime the great cause to which he devoted himself moved steadily on until the Civil War came and all the negroes were set free. Whittier did not believe in war; but when it came he urged the Quakers, who were opposed to fighting, to become nurses, like the nuns and sisters of the Catholic church, and minister to the sick and wounded.

In 1857 the *Atlantic Monthly* was started in

Boston. All the great writers of the day were to have a hand in it—Longfellow, Lowell, Emerson, Holmes, and others. Whittier was also invited to take part, and an edition of his collected poems was published. The *Atlantic Monthly* paid more for contributions than most other periodicals in those days. Whittier got fifty dollars for each poem, and had a poem published nearly every month. He was in very delicate health at this time, and was so poor that this small amount was a godsend to him. He did not attend the monthly dinners in Boston, to which all the other literary men went, for he was a Quaker and did not approve of wine and luxuries; and besides he was not well enough to go. He sent his poems, however, with modest little notes, asking Lowell if he thought they would do, and telling him not to hesitate in rejecting them if he thought them silly. He seemed always to be afraid lest his beautiful simple poems would be so simple that some people would consider them foolish.

In 1858 his mother died, and now he lived

alone with his sister. She, too, died in 1864, the last year of the war, and the next year he wrote ''Snow-Bound'' as a sort of tribute to her memory. It was published in Boston in 1866 and at once proved very popular. Whittier made $10,000 out of the royalties on it. His great regret was that his mother and sister had not lived to enjoy the benefit of his good fortune.

Two famous poems deserve mention. One is '' Barbara Frietchie.'' A lady friend of Whittier heard the story in Washington, and at once said, '' That is a beautiful subject for a ballad by Whittier. It is almost like a scrap of paper lying around with his signature on it.'' So she wrote it out and sent it to him. Not long after that he wrote the poem, following the original story almost exactly. Some people afterward declared that it was not true; but there was certainly an old German woman who kept the Union flag waving over the rebel troops.

The other poem is ''The Barefoot Boy.'' Whittier wrote it in memory of his own boyhood. ''For,'' says he, ''I was once a barefoot boy.'' It pleased him very much, and he sent it up to Mr. Fields, who was then editing the *Atlantic*, and asked "if he thought it would do." Mr. Fields thought it very fine, and said it must go into the edition of Whittier's works which he was then publishing.

Whittier was now sixty years old. The struggles of war and politics were over. The dear ones he loved were dead. To amuse and relieve himself he wrote those simple, beautiful ballads, which every person has read and admired. They were among the finest things he ever did. Among them were "Maud Muller," "Skipper Ireson's Ride," and others equally familiar. They were cheerful and happy, and some were about the days of his childhood. There was occasionally a tinge of sadness in them, but sadness mingled with hope.

Of all sad words of tongue or pen,
The saddest are these: "It might have been!"

Ah, well! for us all some sweet hope lies
Deeply buried from human eyes;

And, in the hereafter, angels may
Roll the stone from its grave away!

Whittier's life *might have been* much easier and much happier. But he had helped much in the accomplishment of a great work, and he was not one to regret all his hardships and sufferings.

CHAPTER XII

THE END OF A SUCCESSFUL LIFE

Before closing this short biography we must refer briefly to one or two interesting anecdotes and circumstances. Whittier was color-blind, at least as to red and green. He could see no difference between the color of ripe strawberries and the leaves of the vine. Yellow he thought the finest color in the world, and perhaps for this reason he preferred the golden-rod.

When the Peace Jubilee was to be celebrated after the Civil War, Patrick S. Gilmore, the famous bandmaster, asked Whittier to write an ode for the occasion. He declined, and then Gilmore offered a prize to the poet who would contribute the best one. Whittier thought he would write one and send it anonymously. No notice was taken of it. Some people will point a moral to this tale by saying, "See what a reputation is!"

Whittier was very fond of pets. Once he had a gray parrot. It was trained on shipboard and would swear occasionally; but it soon fell into the quiet ways of its home. One Sunday morning, however, it got on top of the chimney while the church bells were ringing, and began to dance and scream and swear, while the poor Quakers inside the house came out and looked helplessly up at him, wondering how they would get him down. After that he fell down the chimney and remained in the soot two days. When he was discovered and taken out he was nearly starved, and died not long after.

Whittier also had a little bantam rooster which he trained to crow when he placed it at the door of his niece's room in the morning. Every morning Whittier would push open her door and put the rooster on top of it; and the little fowl would crow lustily until his young mistress was quite awake.

One day not long after the war the Whittiers received a small box, and on opening it they were astonished to see little spikes sticking out all over. Whittier's niece at once guessed it must be an infernal machine, and took it out and buried it in the garden. A few days after there came a letter saying a paperweight, made out of the bullets from a famous battlefield, had been sent. Then they knew it must be the thing they thought an infernal machine, and went and dug it up; and after that it always stood on the poet's desk.

During the time of the war, Gail Hamilton, a friend of Whittier's, embroidered a pair of slippers for him. They were in Quaker gray, but on them was pictured a fierce eagle, with a bunch of thunderbolts in one claw. He was looking knowingly around, as much as to say that if he got a good chance when nobody was looking, he would hurl those thunderbolts. This was intended as a joke on Whittier, who was a Quaker and opposed to war, but still had a good deal of the warlike spirit in him ready to break out at any moment. Whittier used to say, referring to the slippers, that Gail Hamilton was as sharp with her needle as with her tongue.

On the occasion of his seventieth birthday, Whittier was given a great dinner at the Hotel Brunswick in Boston. Nearly all the famous writers of the day were present. When it came the poet's turn to respond to the address of congratulation, he said Longfellow would read a short poem he had written. He handed a paper to that poet, who read the response.

After that, his birthdays were celebrated more or less regularly, and often Whittier had to make great efforts to escape the "pilgrims" who came to Amesbury to see him. Once a party of boys from Exeter Academy started over to visit him and get his autograph. By accident they were delayed, and when they reached his house it was the dead of night and the poet was in bed. He got up, however, and gave them hospitality, writing in all their books. Before he had finished, one of the boys said, "You have written only John in my book."

"I am afraid some of you haven't even got as much as that," said he drily, and took up the candle and went off to bed.

He died on the 7th of September, 1892, at the house of some friends in New Hampshire, with whom he was staying.

We cannot close this account of the life of the dearest and sweetest of poets better than by quoting his own words about himself:

> And while my words are read,
> Let this at least be said:
> "Whate'er his life's defeatures,
> He loved his fellow-creatures.
>
> .   .   .   .   .   .
>
> "To all who humbly suffered,
> His tongue and end he offered;
> His life was not his own,
> Nor lived for self alone.
>
> "Hater of din and riot,
> He lived in days unquiet;
> And, lover of all beauty,
> Trod the hard ways of duty.

"He meant no wrong to any,
He sought the good of many,
Yet knew both sin and folly,—
May God forgive him wholly!"

Also these lines from "My Soul and I":

I have wrestled stoutly with the wrong,
    And borne the right
From beneath the footfall of the throng
    To life and light.

Wherever Freedom shivered a chain,
    God speed, quoth I;
To Error amidst her shouting train
    I gave the lie.

NOTE.—The thanks of the publishers are due Messrs. Houghton, Mifflin & Co. for their kind permission to use selections from the copyrighted works of Whittier.

THE STORY OF

OLIVER WENDELL HOLMES

OLIVER WENDELL HOLMES

HOLMES

CHAPTER I

THE TRUE HUMORIST

Oliver Wendell Holmes was the humorist among American poets, always with a smile around his mouth and a twinkle in his eye, and a kindly little half-hidden joke in everything he had to say. He was a humorist of the genuine good-humored sort, the "genial Autocrat," the kindly and obliging friend (for did he not write a poem on every possible occasion at the request of all sorts of people?) How kind, how pathetic, yet how amusing, are the sweet, quaint lines of "The Last Leaf":

> My grandmamma has said—
> Poor old lady, she is dead
> Long ago—
> That he had a Roman nose,
> And his cheek was like a rose
> In the snow;

195

But now his nose is thin,
And it rests upon his chin
    Like a staff;
And a crook is in his back,
And a melancholy crack
    In his laugh.

I know it is a sin
For me to sit and grin
    At him here;
But the old three-cornered hat,
And the breeches, and all that,
    Are so queer!

And if I should live to be
The last leaf upon the tree
    In the spring,
Let them smile, as I do now,
At the old forsaken bough
    Where I cling.

Dear Doctor Holmes! He did indeed live to be
the last leaf upon the tree ; but to the very end he
went scattering his humorous and good-humored
words among his friends wherever he was, making
people happier as well as wiser, more light-hearted

as well as more thoughtful, until they turned from crying to laughing. " The Last Leaf " is a little sad, notwithstanding its lightness and fun. But there is no sadness in this, the funniest poem that Holmes ever wrote:

THE HEIGHT OF THE RIDICULOUS

I wrote some lines once on a time
  In wondrous merry mood,
And thought, as usual, men would say
  They were exceeding good.

They were so queer, so very queer,
  I laughed as I would die;
Albeit in the general way,
  A sober man am I.

I called my servant, and he came;
  How kind it was of him
To mind a slender man like me,
  He of the mighty limb!

"These to the printer," I exclaimed,
  And, in my humorous way,
I added (as a trifling jest),
  "There 'll be the devil to pay."

He took the paper, and I watched,
  And saw him peep within;
At the first line he read, his face
  Was all upon the grin.

He read the next, the grin grew broad,
  And shot from ear to ear;
He read the third, a chuckling noise
  I now began to hear.

The fourth, he broke into a roar;
  The fifth, his waistband split;
The sixth, he burst five buttons off,
  And tumbled in a fit.

Ten days and nights, with sleepless eye,
  I watched that wretched man;
And since, I never dare to write
  As funny as I can.

CHAPTER II

THE BIRTH OF OLIVER HOLMES

"In the last week of August used to fall Commencement day at Cambridge," remarks the doctor. "I remember that week well, for something happened to me once at that time, namely, I was born."

It was in the year 1809—the same year that Gladstone, Tennyson, Darwin, and Lincoln were born—and on August 29. There is still in existence an old and yellow almanac that belonged once to Dr. Abiel Holmes, Oliver's father. On the page given to August the numbers of the days run down the left-hand side, 1, 2, 3, down to 28, 29, 30, 31. Opposite 29 are two little parallel lines, used as a star or mark of reference, and at the bottom of the page the two little lines are repeated, and after them is written in ink "*son b.*" Of course "*b*" stands for "born." A few grains of black sand were scattered over the wet ink to prevent it from blotting, and some of those grains of sand may be seen glistening there to this day. Oliver Wendell Holmes was born, and the fact of his birth was thus recorded in the almanac—"*son b.*"

Samuel Johnson was born in 1709; or, as Holmes expresses it, "the year 1709 was made ponderous and illustrious in English history by his birth." It appeared to strike Holmes as a huge joke that

he had been born just one hundred years after Dr.
Johnson, and he amused himself by following out
the parallel of their lives. Every year he used
to take down his copy of Boswell's "Life of Johnson" to see what the big, wise old grumbler was
doing in that year, just a hundred years before.
At last, in the year 1884, when he came to the
end of Johnson's life, he said that he felt that
the incubus was raised; he had outlived the ponderous parallel.

The birth of the "laughing philosopher," as
Holmes has been called, took place in a very old
house in Cambridge, close to Harvard College, and
made famous in his poems as "the old ·gambrel-
roofed house." After the battle of Lexington,
General-in-chief Artemas Ward had made this
house the headquarters for the rallying of the
patriots, and General Warren had stopped there
on his way to Bunker Hill. George Washington
and other famous men in those days must often
have darkened its doors.

For years it stood, this quaint old house in which
Holmes was born and grew to manhood, and from

which he went to Harvard College; but before he died the property was sold to the University and the house was torn down. Holmes admitted that it was "a case of justifiable domicide." He went to pay it a last visit, and "found a ghost in each and every chamber and closet," and to each he said a fond goodbye. When the land was leveled down he did not care to go that way again.

Oliver's father, Dr. Abiel Holmes, was an orthodox clergyman of the strictest kind. But he was nearly as good-natured as his son. He was a handsome young man, and all the girls used to say, "There goes Holmes—look!"

Colonel Thomas Wentworth Higginson once found a letter written by his mother when she was a girl, in which she gives some gossip about Dr. Abiel. He sent it to his friend Oliver Wendell and you can imagine the doctor's amusement when he read the following paragraph:

"Now, mamma, I am going to surprise you. Mr. Abiel Holmes, of Cambridge, whom we so kindly chalked out for Miss N. W., is going to be married and, of all folks in the world, guess who to! Miss Sally Wendell! I am sure you will not believe it. However, it is an absolute fact, for Harriet and M. Jackson told Miss P. Russell so, who told us; it has been kept secret for six weeks, nobody knows for what. I could not believe it for some time, and scarcely can now; however, it is a fact, they say."

Evidently girls a hundred years ago wrote much as they do now.

CHAPTER III

AN AMERICAN ARISTOCRAT

Oliver Wendell Holmes belonged to one of the most aristocratic families of Boston, and he seemed proud of it. But he was an aristocrat of the right sort. Said he: "I go for the man with the family portraits against the one with the twenty-cent daguerreotype, *unless* I find out that the latter is the better of the two." He said also: "I like to see worthless rich people yield their places to deserving poor ones, who, beginning with sixpence or nothing, come out at last on

Beacon street and have the sun come into their windows all the year round."

He inherited good blood through three lines, each of which was represented in his own name. The Oliver represents his Boston "blue blood," which came to him from both his father's and his mother's family. One of his ancestors was Lieutenant-Governor Andrew Oliver, the distributor of stamps in Boston, whom the people hated so, though he was one of the richest of the old Bostonians, had coaches, a chariot, and negro slaves, as well as good sterling silver plate that exists in the Holmes and Oliver families to this day.

The Wendell stands for the old Dutch family of Wendells, who had moved from Albany to Boston, and who came originally from Embden, in East Friesland, just on the border line between Germany and the Netherlands. The Wendells are still a wealthy and influential family in Albany, solid old Dutch burghers. Two of Dr. Holmes's Dutch ancestors were shoemakers ; one was a fur trader.

Another of Holmes's forefathers on his mother's side was Governor Thomas Dudley, of whom the famous Cotton Mather wrote these verses :

"In books a prodigal, they say;
A living cyclopedia ;
Of histories of church and priest,
A full compendium, at least ;
A table-talker, rich in sense,
And witty without wit's pretense."

Governor Dudley's daughter, Mrs. Anne Bradstreet, from whom Holmes was descended, was the first American poet. In 1650 she published the first volume of verse ever written by an American. It came out in London, and was entitled "The Tenth Muse Lately Sprung Up in America," and so popular was it that it went through eight editions. Among the other descendants of this first American poetess were William Ellery Channing and Wendell Phillips.

The first Holmes in the genealogy was a lawyer of Gray's Inn, London. John Holmes was born near Boston, and went in 1686 to help settle Woodstock, Connecticut. Holmes's great-grand-mother Bathsheba, the wife of David Holmes, was a most remarkable lady. She was famous as a doctor and nurse.

They tell a fine story of her daring, how once, in 1717, when the snow almost buried the houses after a terrible storm, she climbed out of the upper window of her house in Woodstock and traveled on snowshoes over hill and dale to Dudley, Massachusetts, to attend a sick woman. She was accompanied by two men, who held the ends of a long pole, while she held on in the middle.

There is another remarkable story told of her. Those were the days of Indian massacres. When the men went out to work they took their guns with them, leaving the women in the fort or garrison house.

Once the women when alone asked, ''Who will go to the garden for vegetables?'' Bathsheba Holmes alone dared venture out. She got her vegetables and came back, but not until years afterward did she know in what danger she had been. Then a solitary, decrepit Indian, broken in spirit, called at her door to beg for cider, promising to tell her a story if he got his drink.

She gave him the cider and he told his story. It related to the brave lady herself. He said that when she went to the garden for vegetables, on that occasion long ago, he had been hidden in the woods and had seen her, and had determined to kill her. He had bent his bow and aimed his arrow well, and in a moment he would have let it fly; but a mysterious power stayed his arm; he couldn't shoot. When she had gone safely into the garden he called himself a coward and determined to have her life when she came out. But, as she passed on her way back to the fort, the same power stayed his arm again, and he wondered that he could not kill a squaw. He had always thought that it was the Great Spirit who held his arm and saved her life. It was in this mysterious way that God preserved the line that was finally to give us the "genial autocrat," the "good doctor."

Our poet's grandfather Holmes was a captain in the French and Indian war, and a surgeon in the Revolution, dying a year or two before the close of the latter war.

So you see what a thorough aristocrat, of the true American kind, Oliver Wendell Holmes was.

CHAPTER IV

CAMBRIDGE

Holmes, the poet, was born and brought up in a poetic town. The old, yellow, hip-roofed house stood close beside the grounds of Harvard College; and all around were homes of men who were famous or were to be famous. Cambridge has always been a quaint, quiet, peaceful, well-bred town. It stands at the back door of Boston, a half hour's walk from that "hub of the solar system." Elms and poplars line its streets, its houses look like rich old relics, and everywhere are evidences of comfort and culture. Imagine how George Washington and General Warren, and all the Revolutionary heroes walked up and down these streets! Already in the time of Washington many famous people had lived there; and after him came a whole procession of great men, one after another—Longfellow, Emerson, Sumner, Garrison, Motley—their names are too many to mention.

In the center of the town are the Harvard College buildings, of brick and stone, some old, some new, surrounded by broad green lawns, and some of them overrun with ivy. Then, running out from the college grounds as a hub, are streets like the spokes of a wheel. In one direction is Mount Auburn cemetery, where hundreds of the famous dead lie buried, and which is the most beautiful cemetery in the United States. In another direction are Lexington and Concord, while on another side the Charles River flows serenely along towards Boston Bay.

Everywhere about are to be seen college students and professors. Here is a dapper young man with a pointed beard — the new professor of English; there is a bent old man, white-haired, tottering in his gait—he is the famous professor of Greek. Some of the students are gay and always cracking jokes; others have deepset eyes and shabby clothes—"plugs" the others call them, for they are very serious minded young fellows and never waste a moment of time. Then there are many more who go singing and shouting through the streets at late hours in the night, causing the people who are abed and asleep to be aroused from their slumbers ʌ only to stick their heads out of the windows and silently wish the young fellows were anywhere but in Cambridge.

Such is this famous college town; and a very enjoyable place it is to live in. A great many famous people come here to preach in the churches, or to lecture, or to speak at banquets and meetings. A great many pretty girls come here to see the sights and visit their brothers—and look at the crowds of handsome young men.

In this old college town, this young aristocrat, the descendant of patriots and governors and men of wealth and women of beauty, grew quietly up to manhood. He went to school, learned his lessons well, but not too well, never got into trouble, had a good time, and did not fret or worry about anything, or annoy anybody, even his teachers.

There is a story of a famous feruling that he got—
only one—and years afterward the teacher came to
him to apologize. Holmes in a letter tells in his
humorous way how the repentant master came and
introduced himself to the now famous poet, how in
an embarrassed manner he recalled old days, and
finally the feruling, and then said he was sorry he
had given it. Holmes declared he had richly deserved it; but the schoolmaster was glad to get
away. Apologizing to a pupil for whipping him is
indeed an embarrassing thing.

It was not at school, however, but in his father's
library that Oliver learned most. That room in
the corner of the old house where were the dents
of the British muskets, was the study, and it was
filled from floor to ceiling, every wall, with books.
He says he "bumped about among books from the
time when he was hardly taller than one of his
father's or grandfather's folios."

Beside the library, there was the old garden,
which he himself has quaintly described. "There
were old lilac bushes at the right of the entrance,
and in the corner at the left that remarkable moral

pear tree which gave me one of my first lessons in life. Its fruit never ripened, but always rotted at the core just before it began to grow mellow. It was a vulgar specimen at best, and was set there no doubt to preach its annual sermon. But in the northern border was a high-bred Saint Michael pear tree, which taught a lesson that all of gentle blood might take to heart; for its fruit used to get hard and dark, and break into unseemly cracks, so that when the lord of the harvest came for it, it was like those rich men's sons we see too often, who have never ripened, but only rusted, hardened, and shrunken. We had peaches, lovely nectarines, and sweet white grapes, growing and coming to kindly maturity in those days.

"As for the garden beds, they were cared for by the Jonathan or Ephraim of the household, sometimes assisted by one Rube, a little old Scotch gardener, with a stippled face and a lively temper. Nothing but old-fashioned flowers in them — hyacinths pushing their green beaks through as soon as the snow was gone, or earlier; tulips, coming up in the shapes of cornucopiæ; peonies, butting their blunt way through the loosened earth; lilies, roses—damask, white, blush, cinnamon; larkspurs, lupines, and gorgeous hollyhocks.

".The yellow-birds used to be very fond of some sunflowers that grew close to the pear tree with a moral. I remember their flitting about, golden in the golden light, over the golden flowers, as if they were flakes of curdled sunshine."

Oliver had a younger brother John, who was as light of heart and full of fun as he; and gay times they had together in this quiet old town, and this old house with its books and its garden. He says that as a boy he was afraid of the tall masts of ships that used to come up the river, and he would hide his eyes from them. And he was afraid, too, of a great wooden hand, the sign of a glove-maker whose shop he sometimes passed.

So in happiness and comfort he dreamed his early years away, with his brothers and sisters and father and mother. He was like a fine, luscious pear in that old garden, ripening without rotting at the core, or yet getting hard and full of cracks.

CHAPTER V

SCHOOL LIFE

When young Oliver was ten, he was sent about a mile away to a school where one of the pupils was Margaret Fuller, who afterwards became a famous writer. As a girl, says Holmes, she had the reputation of being "smart." Once she wrote a school essay which was shown to the father of Oliver. It began, "It is a *trite* remark." But Oliver didn't know what *trite* meant. It was to him a crushing discovery of her superiority. She was stately and distant, as if she had great thoughts of her own; she was a diligent student, and read a great many of what she called "naw-vels." "A remarkable point about her," says Holmes, "was that long, flexile neck, arching and undulating in strange sinuous movements, which one who loved her compared to those of a swan, and one who loved her not to the serpent that tempted Eve."

After five years at this school, Oliver was taken to Andover, and left at the house of a professor in the theological seminary. He went to Phillips

Academy, where he studied a year preparatory to entering Harvard College. There he met a rosy-faced boy named Phineas Barnes, and the two became great friends. Phineas did not go to Harvard College, and they were soon separated; but they always remained friends, and kept up a correspondence as long as they lived.

At this time, says one of his biographers, he was an energetic and lively youngster, full of fun and mischief, with tendencies in the way of flageolets and flutes, and with a weakness for pistols and guns and cigars, which latter he would hide in the barrel of the pistol, where his mother's eyes would never care to look for them.

One of the objects of most interest to the boys at this school was a tutor who had had a dream that he would fall dead while he was praying. He regarded the dream as a warning, and asked the boys to come in turn to see him before he died. Says Holmes, "More than one boy kept his eye on him during his devotions, possessed by the same feeling the man had who followed Van Amburgh about with the expectation, let us not say hope, of seeing the lion bite his head off sooner or later."

Years later he revisited these scenes. He says that the ghost of a boy was at his side as he wandered among the places he knew so well: " 'Two tickets for Boston,' I said to the man at the station.

"But the little ghost whispered, 'When you leave this place you will leave me behind you.'

" 'One ticket for Boston, if you.please. Goodbye, little ghost.' "

At last Holmes returned to Cambridge and immediately entered Harvard College, in "the famous class of '29." He had many well-known classmates, among them the Rev. Samuel Francis Smith, the Rev. Dr. James Freeman Clarke, and others. Smith was afterwards famous as the author of "My Country, 'Tis of Thee," and Dr. Holmes, in one of his poems, thus writes about him:

And there's a nice youngster of excellent pith,—
Fate tried to conceal him by naming him Smith;
But he shouted a song for the brave and the free,—
Just read on his medal, 'My country' 'of thee!'

Charles Sumner was in the next class below, and the famous historian Motley two classes below. Though Motley was the youngest student in the college, he and Holmes afterward became the most intimate of friends, and so remained through life; and when Motley was dead Holmes wrote his biography.

Holmes said Motley looked the ideal of a young poet, and he goes on to describe him: "His finely shaped and expressive features, his large, luminous eyes, his dark waving hair, the singularly spirited set of his head, his well outlined figure, gave promise of manly beauty."

After this description of Motley, read the following which Holmes gives of himself in a letter to Phineas Barnes:

"I, Oliver Wendell Holmes, Junior in Harvard University, am a plumeless biped of exactly five feet three inches when standing in a pair of substantial boots made by Mr. Russell of this town, having eyes which I call blue, and hair which I do not know what to call.

"Secondly, with regard to my moral qualities,

I am rather lazy than otherwise, and certainly do not study as hard as I ought to. I am not dissipated and I am not sedate, and when I last ascertained my college rank I stood in the humble situation of seventeenth scholar."

In another letter written when in college to his friend Phineas he says:

"'What do I do?' I read a little, study a little, smoke a little, and eat a good deal. 'What do I think?' I think that's a deuced hard question. 'What have I been doing these three years?' Why, I have been growing a little in body, and I hope in mind; I have been learning a little of almost everything, and a good deal of some things."

And in still another letter, he says: "I have been writing poetry like a madman, and then I have been talking sentiment like a turtle-dove, and gadding about among the sweet faces, and doing all such silly things that spoil you for everything else. This month of May is too good for anything but love."

CHAPTER VI

COLLEGE LIFE

Holmes was not only born within the present grounds of Harvard, he grew up there, was a student of Harvard, and a loyal member of the "famous class of '29," a lecturer and professor at Harvard, and he became Harvard's most famous poet and man of letters, though Harvard has had so many that were great. So the life at Harvard College was always a part of his life; and perhaps that is why he was so merry.

College students are great jokers. In the days of Holmes the students decidedly objected to going to chapel early in the morning, rising as they had to do before daylight on cold winter days. To show that they didn't like this idea of early prayers, they would sometimes fasten firecrackers to the lids of the big Bible, so that when the president or a professor came to lead the exercises and opened the book, they would go off with a snap.

In those days, too, they had only candles, and as prayers were held before daylight the chapel candles had to be lighted. Sometimes the students would put pieces of lead where the wick ought to be, and when the candles burned down to the lead the lights went out, of course leaving the chapel in darkness. At other times the president would be startled on entering the pulpit by seeing a pig's head standing upright and bristly on his desk.

The rooms in the college dormitories were very poorly furnished. Instead of matches they had flint and steel and a tinder-box; and in almost every room was a cannon ball, which the boys would heat red-hot and set on a metal frame of some sort to help keep the room warm. Sometimes in the middle of the night a wicked student or two would send one of these cannon balls rolling, bump, bump, bump, down the stairs, waking every one and getting the proctor out of bed. Sometimes, too, the cannon ball was hot and burned the fingers of the proctor when he tried to pick it up. Then woe to the young lad who was caught and proved to be the culprit.

In college, Holmes belonged to two or three

clubs.   One was the Hasty Pudding Club, which
met in the rooms of the members.   A worthy old
lady of the village called Sister Stimson prepared
the pudding in two huge pots; and the "providers"
of the evening would sling these, filled with the
boiling mush, on a stout pole, and, resting the ends
upon their shoulders, mount gallantly to the room
where the members were assembled, often in the
third or fourth story.   A bowl of hasty pudding
was always carried to the officer in the entry, as a
sort of peace offering; and when the members had
eaten as much as they could, and had told all the
stories they had to tell, the occupants of nearby
rooms were invited to help finish up the repast,

Another club to which he belonged was called the
" Med. Facs.," and each member or officer had the
title of a supposed professor in the Medical Faculty
of the University.   The first meeting of the year
was held in an upper room, draped in black cotton
and decorated with death's-heads and cross-bones
in chalk; a table, also hung in black, extended
lengthwise through the room.   In the center sat
the mock president and about him were the "pro-

fessors" and "assistant professors," all in black. Near at hand stood two policemen, usually the two strongest men in the class, dressed in flesh-colored tights. On the stairs outside were crowds of Juniors, from which twenty or thirty were to be initiated into the society. This initiation consisted usually in answering disagreeable questions put by the "professors," or in doing such things as standing on one's head, crawling about the floor, singing Mother Goose melodies, or making a Latin or Greek oration.

College Commencement in those days was like a country fair. The people pitched tents on the western side of the college yard (for there were then no hotels, and boarding was expensive), and opposite them were various stands and shows, making a street which by nightfall was paved with watermelon rinds, peachstones, and various refuse, on a ground of straw,—all flavored with rum and tobacco smoke.

Holmes himself has well described this festival of the college year:

"The fair plain (the Common), not then, as now,

cut up into cattle pens by the ugliest of known fences, swarmed with the joyous crowds. The ginger-beer carts rang their bells and popped their bottles, the fiddlers played Money Musk over and over and over, the sailors danced the double-shuffle, the gentlemen of the city capered in rusty jigs, the town ladies even took a part in the lusty exercise, the confectioners rattled red and white sugar plums, long sticks of candy, sugar and burnt almonds into their brass scales, the wedges of pie were driven into splitting mouths, the mountains of (clove-sprinkled) hams were cut down as Fort Hill is being sliced to-day; the hungry feeders sat still and concentrated about the boards where the grosser viands were served, while the milk flowed from cracking cocoanûts, the fragrant muskmelons were cloven into new-moon crescents, and the great water-melons showed their cool pulps sparkling and roseate as the dewy fingers of Aurora."

And besides all this, there were the orations of the students, and the speeches of old graduates who now came back famous, and all the bustle and importance of the college men themselves, hurrying to entertain their fair lady friends, their mothers, and their fathers, who had come up to see how they behaved.

CHAPTER VII

A BUDDING POET

We have already seen in one of Holmes's letters to Phineas Barnes that while in college he was "writing poetry like mad." In the appendix to the latest complete edition of his poems you will find some lines translated from the Æneid while he was a student at Andover, not yet sixteen years old. In college he was poet to the Hasty Pudding Club; had a poem at Exhibition, one at Commencement, and was elected class poet; besides that, he joined several classmates in a volume of satirical poems on the first regular art exhibition in Boston.

When he finished his college course he studied law for a year, though his father rather wished him to be a clergyman. Says he, "I might have been a clergyman myself, for aught I know, if a certain clergyman had not looked and talked so like an undertaker." Think of the little smooth-voiced joker in the pulpit! In another place he says, "How grandly the procession of old clergymen who filled our pulpit from time to time, and passed the day under our roof, marches before my closed eyes!" You must remember that Holmes was the son of the orthodox clergyman of Cambridge, and these were the men who exchanged pulpits with his father.

At first, as an experiment, he studied law for a year; but he did not work very hard. He was writing poetry. A paper called the *Collegian* was started, and he contributed twenty-five or more poems to it, among which were some of his funniest and best. "The Last Leaf" and "The Height of the Ridiculous" were among the work of that first poetic year of his. He never thought much of these poems, though some people consider them quite as good as the poems of the famous Thomas Hood, who wrote—

> "Take her up tenderly,
>   Lift her with care,—
> Fashioned so slenderly,
>   Young and so fair!"

Because he didn't like them, or thought them too rollicking, he did not reprint many of them. Here is one, perhaps the first of his poems ever printed with his name, which appeared in February, 1830, under the title "Runaway Ballad":

I

Wake from thy slumbers, Isabel, the stars are in the sky,
And night has hung her silver lamp, to light her altar by;
The flowers have closed their faded leaves, and drooped
  upon the plain;
Oh! wake thee, and their dying hues shall blush to life
  again.

II

Get up! get up! Miss Polly Jones, the tandem's at the
  door;
Get up and shake your lovely bones, it's twelve o'clock
  and more;
The chaises they have rattled by, and nothing stirs around,
And all the world but you and me are snoring safe and
  sound.

III

I've got my uncle's bay, and trotting Peggy, too,
I've lined their tripes with oats and hay, and now for love
  and you!

The lash is curling in the air, and I am at your side;
To-morrow you are Mrs. Snaggs, my bold and blooming
    bride.

Here is another, entitled "Romance":

Oh! she was a maid of a laughing eye,
    And she lived in a garret cold and high;
    And he was a threadbare, whiskered beau,
    And he lived in a cellar damp and low.

But not all his early poems were nonsense like
these. One day, in the fall of 1830, he read in the
Boston Advertiser a paragraph saying that the
Navy Department at Washington intended to
break up the frigate Constitution, which had
fought so bravely in the War of 1812, and won
such glory for the American people. Immediately
he wrote the following poem, which stands at the
beginning of his collected works:

OLD IRONSIDES.

Ay, tear her tattered ensign down!
    Long has it waved on high,
And many an eye has danced to see
    The banner in the sky;

Beneath it rung the battle shout,
  And burst the cannon's roar;—
The meteor of the ocean air
  Shall sweep the clouds no more.

Her deck, once red with heroes' blood,
  Where knelt the vanquished foe,
When winds were hurrying o'er the flood
  And waves were white below,
No more shall feel the victor's tread
  Or know the conquered knee; —
The harpies of the shore shall pluck
  The eagle of the sea!

Oh, better that her shattered hulk
  Should sink beneath the wave;
Her thunders shook the mighty deep,
  And there should be her grave;
Nail to the mast her holy flag,
  Set every threadbare sail,
And give her to the god of storms,
  The lightning and the gale!

This stirring poem was published on the next
day but one, and was immediately copied into
nearly every newspaper in the United States.
Copies were even printed as handbills and distrib-

uted about the city of Washington. Because
the people felt so badly about it, the Navy
Department at last decided not to break up Old
Ironsides.

CHAPTER VIII

DOCTOR HOLMES

Young Mr. Holmes wrote so much poetry he
had little time for law during the twelve months
after his graduation. So at the end of the year
he gave up law and began to study medicine. At
first he felt his heart come up into his throat at
the sight of skeletons grinning at him from the
walls; and his cheek grew pale as the hospital
sheets when he passed among the sufferers and
saw the dead and dying, or helped to perform a
surgical operation ; but after a time these things
were to him as nothing, mere every-day affairs.

About the same time, too, he became a collector
of rare old books. In 1833, when he had finished
his medical education as far as he could at home,
he went to Europe to complete his studies in the

hospitals of Paris and other cities. He remained there two years and a half, and in that time he had a chance to pick up some rare and queer old volumes.

He returned a full-fledged doctor; but he seems to have felt that he had neglected poetry long enough, and soon published his first book, which is dated 1836. He had been invited to read a long and serious poem before the Phi Beta Kappa society of Harvard, and this he made the chief poem of his little volume, including more than forty others. Beside the early humorous poems which we have already referred to, there was the well-known poem "The September Gale," beginning, —

> I'm not a chicken; I have seen
> Full many a chill September,—

and ending, —

> And not till fate has cut the last
> Of all my earthly stitches,
> This aching heart shall cease to mourn
> My loved, my long-lost breeches !

George Ticknor Curtis describes the youtnful poet in the following bright paragraph:

"Dr. Holmes had then just returned from Europe. Extremely youthful in his appearance, bubbling over with the mingled humor and pathos that have always marked his poetry, and sparkling with coruscations of his peculiar genius, his Phi Beta Kappa poem of 1836, delivered with a clear, ringing enunciation, which imparted to the hearers his own enjoyment of his thoughts and expressions, delighted a cultivated audience to a very uncommon degree."

Here is another description of the reading of the same poem, which was printed in *The Atlantic Monthly:*

"A brilliant, airy, and *spirituelle* manner, varied with striking flexibility to the changing sentiment of the poem,—now deeply impassioned, now gayly joyous and nonchalant, and anon springing up almost into an actual flight of rhapsody,—rendered the delivery of this poem a rich, nearly a dramatic, entertainment, such as we have rarely witnessed."

Abraham Lincoln read and admired the poems in this first little volume. Once, in conversation, he remarked, "There are some quaint, queer verses, written, I think, by Oliver Wendell Holmes, entitled 'The Last Leaf,' one of which is to me inexpressibly touching." He then repeated the poem from memory, and as he finished this much-admired stanza,—

> The mossy marbles rest
> On the lips that he has prest
> In their bloom ;
> And the names he loved to hear
> Have been carved for many a year
> On the tomb,—

he said, "For pure pathos, in my judgment, there is nothing finer than those six lines in the English language." Perhaps Lincoln was thinking of the lonely grave of his own first love in Illinois, for he once said, "Oh, I cannot bear the thought of her lying out there with the storms beating upon her."

Holmes, having received his degree of M. D. from Harvard College, began practicing medicine in Boston. He was young and popular, he was related to the best families, and he had the best medical education the world could give. The result was that he had plenty of practice. He didn't believe much in giving medicine, and his doses were usually very small. He would enter the sick-room with a bright, cheerful smile on his face that of itself made the patient soon feel better. In one of his books he gives this maxim : "When visiting a patient enter the sick-room at once, without keeping the patient in the torture of suspense by discussing the case with others in another room."

Prize medals were offered in Boston for medical essays, and in the first two years after he began practicing medicine he gained three of these medals. In 1838, after two years in Boston, he was appointed professor of anatomy and physiology in Dartmouth College. He remained there two years, at the end of which time he resigned. He then came back to Boston and married the daughter of Judge Charles Jackson. He and his wife took a house in the very heart of Boston, in a little court leading out of Tremont street, and there they lived for nearly twenty years. "When he first entered that house two shadows glided over the threshold; five lingered in the doorway when he passed through it for the last time,—and one of the shadows was claimed by its owner to be longer than his own." Those other shadows were his children, his eldest son being taller than the doctor himself. In the surrounding houses there had been sorrow and disappointment and death. "The whole drama of life was played in that stock company's theatre of a dozen houses, one of which was his, and no deep sorrow or severe calamity ever entered his dwelling. Peace be to those walls, forever," the professor said, "for the many pleasant years he has passed within them."

He had two sons and a daughter. The oldest son was named Oliver Wendell, and became a judge. The other son, Edward, was also a lawyer. The daughter, named after his wife Amelia Jackson, married Mr. John Turner Sargent, and it was at her country home at Beverly Farms that

Holmes spent much of his time toward the end of his life.

He practiced medicine again in Boston for seven years, when he accepted an appointment as professor of anatomy and physiology in Harvard Medical School. This professorship he held for thirty-five years, when he resigned on account of old age.

He had a beautiful country home called Canoe Place, in the Berkshire Hills, in western Massachusetts. There he spent "seven happy summer vacations, which," he declares, "stand in his memory like the seven golden candlesticks seen in the beatific vision of the holy dreamer." Some famous literary people lived near by, among them Herman Melville, the novelist and traveler, and not far away were Miss Sedgwick and Fanny Kemble, and for a short time Hawthorne. The doctor's dwelling was a modest one, he tells us,— "not glorious, yet not unlovely in the youth of its drab and mahogany,—full of great and little boys' playthings." This place had come to him by inheritance from his mother.

CHAPTER IX

THE AUTOCRAT

In 1852 Holmes delivered a course of lectures on the "English Poets of the Nineteenth Century,"—Wordsworth, Moore, Keats, Shelley, and others. At the end of each lecture he read a poem, and these poems now appear in his collected works as "After a Lecture on Wordsworth," "After a Lecture on Moore," etc.

In a letter to an official he states the terms on which he is willing to give this course of lectures in various towns and cities:

"My terms for a lecture, when I stay over night, are fifteen dollars and expenses, a room with a fire in it, in a public house, and a mattress to sleep on,—not a feather bed. As you write in your individual capacity, I tell you at once all my habitual exigencies. I am afraid to sleep in a cold room ; I can't sleep on a feather bed ; I will not go to private houses ; and I have fixed upon the sum mentioned as what it is worth to go away for the night to places that cannot pay more."

The landlady in the "Autocrat of the Breakfast Table" also has something to say about his
lectures:

"He was a man that loved to stick around
home as much as any cat you ever see in your life.
He used to say he'd as lief have a tooth pulled as
go away anywheres. Always got sick, he said,
when he went away, and never sick when he
didn't. Pretty nigh killed himself goin' about
lecturing two or three winters,—talkin' in cold
country lyceums,—as he used to say,—goin' home
to cold parlors and bein' treated to cold apples and
cold water ; and then goin' up into a cold bed in a
cold chamber, and comin' home next mornin' with
a cold in his head as bad as the horse distemper."

Perhaps this is why Holmes was not more of a
traveler, going to Europe but twice, and hardly
ever leaving his birthplace of Cambridge or his
home in Boston.

So twenty years passed by after he published
his first volume of poems before he did anything
else very literary. His fellow professor Longfellow had become famous ; and so had Haw-

thorne ; and so, too, had Lowell and Whittier. But Holmes seemed to have no desire for fame. He had written a few amusing poems, and delivered some lectures.

But when the *Atlantic Monthly* was about to be started, all the literary folk turned to Holmes and said, "That jolly old fellow could write something good, if he only would."

The young publishers, Phillips & Sampson, were enthusiastic about the new magazine. Lowell was chosen editor, and Francis H. Underwood was assistant, though the idea was originally his. They called in Longfellow and Emerson, and Motley and Holmes. This distinguished company met at a dinner and talked over the new project. Holmes suggested the name *Atlantic Monthly*. Longfellow would contribute a poem now and then, and Emerson an essay from time to time ; but poems and essays do not fill up a magazine very fast. So Lowell determined to get something from Holmes, some light, gossipy prose, that should continue on from month to month. The doctor remembered that he had written some papers twenty-five years before for the *New England Magazine*, and he determined to "shake the same bough again" and see what fruit he could get. So he began where he had left off all those years before with an "As-I-was-saying." And for a year or more, every month in the *Atlantic*, the "Autocrat" gave his opinions of life, cracked his little jokes on men and things, recited a poem, or gossiped with his landlady and fellow boarders. And each month that distinguished literary company met at some hotel or restaurant in Boston and had a dinner which was a feast of reason and good things for the mind and heart as well as for the stomach ; and Holmes was the wit and soul of every banquet.

At last Oliver Wendell Holmes had come before the world as a great poet and a great humorist. The "Autocrat" is the very soul of humor, so genial, so wise in his good advice, so gay in his good nature, so light and sparkling and kind. Now was published "The Deacon's Masterpiece, or, The Wonderful One-Hoss Shay"; and by its side that most beautiful of all the poems Holmes ever wrote, "The Chambered Nautilus." When the Princess of Wales asked him to write in her album, he copied the last verse of "The Chambered Nautilus," as he had done in the album of many a subject of our great republic. Listen! Holmes could be stately and beautiful as well as gay and humorous :

Build thee more stately mansions, O my soul,
  As the swift seasons roll!
  Leave thy low-vaulted past!
Let each new temple, nobler than the last,
Shut thee from heaven with a dome more vast,
  Till thou at length art free,
Leaving thine outgrown shell by life's unresting sea!

If you wish to know the wise things Holmes said about anything and everything, read "The Autocrat of the Breakfast Table." Here are a few bright sayings which you will not find in that book, but which will give you an idea of the kind of things with which the volume is filled :

"An Indian is a few instincts on legs, and holding a tomahawk."

"If a doctor has the luck to find out a new

malady, it is tied to his name like a tin kettle to a dog's tail, and he goes clattering down the highway of fame to posterity with his æolian attachment following at his heels."

Gunpowder : "Chemistry seals up a few dark grains in iron vases, and lo! at the touch of a single spark, rises in smoke and flames a mighty Afrit with a voice like thunder and an arm that shatters like an earthquake."

"The scholar's mind is furnished with shelves like his library. Each book knows its place in the brain as well as against the wall or in the alcove. His consciousness is doubled by the books which encircle him, as the trees that surround a lake repeat themselves in its unruffled waters. Men talk of the nerve that runs to the pocket, but one who loves his books, and has lived long with them, has a nervous filament which runs from his sensorium to every one of them."

"Slang—is the way in which a lazy adult shifts the trouble of finding any exact meaning in his (or her) conversation on the other party. If both talkers are indolent, all their talk lapses into the vague generalities of childhood. It is a prevalent social vice of the time, as it has been of times that are past."

Perhaps the most famous expression in the "Autocrat" is that in which he calls Boston "the hub of the solar system" (often wrongly quoted as "the hub of the universe").

"The Autocrat of the Breakfast Table" was such a success that it sold the *Atlantic Monthly* by the thousands of copies. The editors and publishers both said, "This is just the thing : give us more, give us more." So Holmes wrote another book, which he called "The Professor at the Breakfast Table"; and then "The Poet at the Breakfast Table."

In the "Autocrat" Holmes said that every man had in him the writing of at least one novel. As the demand for his work was great, he thought he would write one. So he produced "Elsie Venner, a Romance of Destiny." It is a strange story of a girl who has the nature of a snake. Holmes had heard of cases like that of Elsie Venner, and he worked her story out in a scientific manner.

We read it as if it were really true, and it exercises a weird fascination over us.

Later he wrote another novel, entitled "The
Guardian Angel."

CHAPTER X

"THE FAMOUS CLASS OF '29"

Holmes was the poet of the occasional, if ever
there was one. If anybody held a meeting about
anything, and Holmes was asked to read a poem,
he kindly consented to do so. Who ever heard of
opening a meeting of a medical society with a poem?
Yet Holmes read an original poem at many a
meeting of the Massachusetts Medical Society.

It was at the yearly meeting of "the famous
class of '29" that he read his poems oftenest.
Every year for sixty years, this loyal poet remained
true to class traditions. A poem from Holmes
was always expected, and the class always got it.

A college class is a band of friends, friends who
have passed the merriest years of their lives
together. They come to college from the country
over, from homes poor and rich, distant and near.

For four years they live together, all on an equal footing, all together blooming into manhood. Then they scatter to their various duties in the world. One is a lawyer, another a journalist, another a clergyman, another a doctor, and others are business men. Yet how can they ever forget those happy years together?

Each year all those members of the class of '29 who could do so would come together at Commencement time to renew old memories. Some of the class were perhaps over seas and in foreign lands; some, alas! were dead. So, as the years passed by, the number grew smaller and smaller, and the gathering became sadder and sadder; yet none of them would have missed it.

The first class poem in Holmes's works is entitled "Bill and Joe," and begins thus:

> Come, dear old comrades, you and I
> Will steal an hour from days gone by,
> The shining days when life was new,
> And all was bright with morning dew,
> The lusty days of long ago,
> When you were Bill and I was Joe.

Most of these verses are of sad memories of happy times gone forever:

> Where, oh, where are the visions of morning,
>   Fresh as the dews of our prime?
> Gone, like the tenants that quit without warning,
>   Down the back entry of time.

.But some are poems of dear friendship and pleasure at seeing friends again, like this, called "Indian Summer":

You'll believe me, dear boys, 'tis a pleasure to rise,
With a welcome like this in your darling old eyes;
To meet the same smiles and to hear the same tone
Which have greeted me oft in the years that have flown.

One poem entitled "The Boys" is well worth remembering, especially the last stanzas:

> Then here's to our boyhood, its gold and its gray!
> The stars of its winter, the dews of its May!
> And when we have done with our life-lasting toys,
> Dear Father, take care of thy children, the Boys!

During the times of the great Civil War the poems were mostly of a patriotic kind. Here, for instance, is the way he opens his poem in 1862, entitled "The Good Ship Union":

> 'Tis midnight: through my troubled dream
>   Loud wails the tempest's cry;
> Before the gale, with tattered sail,
>   A ship goes plunging by.
> What name? Where bound?—The rocks around
>   Repeat the loud halloo.
> —The good ship Union, Southward bound:
>   God help her and her crew !

In 1878 he wrote a poem on "The Last Survivor," which opens with these beautiful lines:

> Yes! the vacant chairs tell sadly we are going, going fast,
> And the thought comes strangely o'er me, Who will live to
>   be the last?

Let us add one more verse, a humorous verse in which the joker pretends he's not so very old:

> I don't think I feel much older; I'm aware I'm rather gray;
> But so are many young folks,—I meet 'em every day.
> I confess I'm more particular in what I eat and drink,
> But one's taste improves with culture; that is all it means,
>   I think.

Can you read as once you used to? Well, the printing is so bad,
No young folks' eyes can read it like the books that once
 we had.

Are you quite as quick of hearing? Please to say that once
 again.

Don't I use plain words, your Reverence? Yes, I often use
 a cane.

*   *   *   *   *   *

Ah, well,—I know—at every age life has a certain charm,—
You're going? Come, permit me please, I beg you'll take
 my arm.

I take your arm! Why take your arm? I'd thank you to
 be told

I'm old enough to walk alone, but not so *very* old.

At last, in 1889, the poems stopped, because
there were so few of the class left, and the meetings were so sad. In 1891, Holmes writes to a
friend: "Our old raft of eighteen-twenty-niners is
going to pieces; for the first time no class-meeting
is called for the 8th of January. I shall try to get
the poor remnant of the class together at my
house; but it is doubtful whether there is life
enough left for a gathering of half a dozen. I
have a very tender feeling to my coevals."

CHAPTER XI

A FEW STRAY FACTS

In 1858 Holmes moved from his house in Montgomery Place to 21 Charles street, near the Charles River; and here he was neighbor to Governor Andrew, the war governor of Massachusetts, and James T. Fields, the publisher. He afterward occupied another house on Charles street, and finally, in 1871, moved to Beacon street, where was his home to the end of his life.

In 1882 he resigned his professorship at Harvard and devoted himself to literary work, writing, after this, his last book of table talks, which he called "Over the Teacups." In 1886 he visited Europe. With the exception of the journey which he took when a young man studying medicine, this was his only trip abroad. He was gone only four months, including the voyage both ways, and spent most of his time in the little isle of Britain. It seemed as if he disliked being long away from home, or even away from Boston.

Dr. Holmes was an ingenious man, and had

many fads and fancies. He was the inventor of the small stereoscope for hand use,—such as those used for looking at photographs. The first one he made himself entirely, all but the lenses, and he often used to say that he might have made a fortune out of this invention if he had patented it. Yet, he seems never to have regretted that he had not done so, thinking perhaps that the public had been the gainer by his loss.

A life-long hobby of his was photography—beginning in the days when this art was not so easy and common as it is now. He became a really skillful artist in it, and made many pictures of the old gambrel-roofed house and scenes about Harvard College, which have been preserved and may prove useful to future historians.

Once he thought he could learn to play on the violin. As a matter of fact, he had no ear for harmony, and could never produce music. Still, he shut himself up in his study and scraped away hour after hour, for two or three winters. At the end of that time he could play two or three simple tunes so that they could be recognized; then he gave it up and never played any more.

One of his fads was the measuring of large trees. When he traveled about the country he always had a measuring tape in his pocket, and this he would stretch around the trunk of every big tree he saw. When he went to England he pulled out his bit of string to see if the giant trees of Old England were as big as the giant trees of New England. He tells with what bated breath and beating, fearful heart he measured one tree in particular in England with a string on which he had measured off the trunk of another big tree in America. "Twenty feet, and a long piece of string left!" he exclaims, when telling of it. "Twenty-one feet—twenty-two—twenty-three,—an extra heart-beat or two,—twenty-four—twenty-five, and six inches over !!"

He finally became so noted as an authority on big trees that he was consulted even by the famous botanist, Professor Asa Gray.

In "The Autocrat of the Breakfast Table" you may read of a slice of a hemlock tree, going

straight to the center, and showing three hundred
and forty-two rings, each ring representing a year
of life. Holmes really had this tree section, and
spent much time sticking pins in at the various
rings, each pin tagged with the date of some event
that was taking place when the ring was forming.

We have already spoken of his love for old
books. In the "Autocrat" he says: "I like
books—I was born and bred among them, and
have the easy feelings, when I get into their presence, that a stable-boy has among horses. I don't
think I undervalue them, either as companions or
instructors." He was not only an expert in judg-
ing an old and beautiful book, but he understood
the art of bookbinding, and sometimes practiced
it. Here is a sentence of his about books that we
should all remember: "Some books are edifices,
to stand as they are built; some are hewn stones,
ready to form a part of future edifices ; some are
quarries, from which stones are to be split for
shaping and after use."

Any one who has read the stirring ballad of
"Old Blue," entitled "How the Old Horse Won

the Bet," will guess that Holmes knew something about horse-racing. What could be more vivid than this:

"Go !"—Through his ears the summons stung
As if a battle-trump had rung;
The slumbering instincts long unstirred
Started at the old familiar word;
It thrills like flame through every limb,—
What means his twenty years to him?
The savage blow his rider dealt
Fell on his hollow flanks unfelt;
The spur that pricked his staring hide
Unheeded tore his bleeding side;
Alike to him are spur and rein,—
He steps a five-year-old again !

One of his most cherished memories was that of seeing the famous steed Plenipotentiary win the Derby; this was when Holmes was in England as a young man; and indeed he knew "a neat, snug hoof, a delicate pastern, a broad haunch, a deep chest, a close ribbed-up barrel, as well as any other man in the town."

Besides these things, he was fond of boxing, of

boating, and other forms of sport; and he knew the fine points about all of these manly pastimes.

You must not think, however, that Holmes was not a hard worker and a careful student. He wrote easily and freely, but revised with the greatest care; and he prepared his college lectures over every year, keeping them up to date while he was constantly studying and reading and learning new things about his profession.

CHAPTER XII

THE END COMES

The life of Oliver Wendell Holmes flowed like a placid river, with scarcely a ripple upon its surface. He was born and grew up and passed all his life near that "hub" he has made so famous, surrounded by throngs of friends, never visited by sorrow, always fortunate, always happy. He found amusement in everything, for he looked on the bright side of life and turned everything into humor. And at last he died, painlessly, serenely, sitting in his chair, having been up and about to the very last day. This final event—we cannot call it sad—occurred October 7, 1894. He was eighty-five years old.

We cannot better close this study of America's most genial poet-humorist than by quoting the following appreciative and most touching lines from an English journal:

"THE AUTOCRAT"

"The Last Leaf!" Can it be true,
We have turned it, and on you,
    Friend of all?
That the years at last have power?
That life's foliage and its flower
    Fade and fall?

Was there one who ever took
From its shelf, by chance, a book
    Penned by you,
But was fast your friend for life,
With one refuge from its strife
    Safe and true?

*   *   *   *   *

Trieste

Trieste Publishing has a massive catalogue of classic book titles. Our aim is to provide readers with the highest quality reproductions of fiction and non-fiction literature that has stood the test of time. The many thousands of books in our collection have been sourced from libraries and private collections around the world.

The titles that Trieste Publishing has chosen to be part of the collection have been scanned to simulate the original. Our readers see the books the same way that their first readers did decades or a hundred or more years ago. Books from that period are often spoiled by imperfections that did not exist in the original. Imperfections could be in the form of blurred text, photographs, or missing pages. It is highly unlikely that this would occur with one of our books. Our extensive quality control ensures that the readers of Trieste Publishing's books will be delighted with their purchase. Our staff has thoroughly reviewed every page of all the books in the collection, repairing, or if necessary, rejecting titles that are not of the highest quality. This process ensures that the reader of one of Trieste Publishing's titles receives a volume that faithfully reproduces the original, and to the maximum degree possible, gives them the experience of owning the original work.

We pride ourselves on not only creating a pathway to an extensive reservoir of books of the finest quality, but also providing value to every one of our readers. Generally, Trieste books are purchased singly - on demand, however they may also be purchased in bulk. Readers interested in bulk purchases are invited to contact us directly to enquire about our tailored bulk rates. Email: customerservice@triestepublishing.com

You May Also Like

ISBN: 9780649692613
Paperback: 120 pages
Dimensions: 6.14 x 0.25 x 9.21 inches
Language: eng

Results of Astronomical Observations Made at the Sydney Observatory, New South Wales, in the Years 1877 and 1878

H. C. Russell

ISBN: 9780649669356
Paperback: 164 pages
Dimensions: 6.14 x 0.35 x 9.21 inches
Language: eng

Persecution and Tolerance: Being the Hulsean Lectures Preached Before the University of Cambridge in 1893-4

Mandell Creighton

You May Also Like

ISBN: 9780649057054
Paperback: 140 pages
Dimensions: 6.14 x 0.30 x 9.21 inches
Language: eng

The University of Minnesota. The Calendar for the Year 1883-84

University Minneapolis

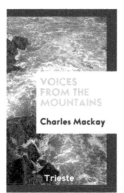

ISBN: 9780649730360
Paperback: 140 pages
Dimensions: 5.25 x 0.30 x 8.0 inches
Language: eng

Voices from the Mountains

Charles Mackay

www.triestepublishing.com

You May Also Like

ISBN: 9780649420544
Paperback: 108 pages
Dimensions: 6.14 x 0.22 x 9.21 inches
Language: eng

1807-1907 The One Hundredth Anniversary of the incorporation of the Town of Arlington Massachusetts

Various

ISBN: 9780649194292
Paperback: 44 pages
Dimensions: 6.14 x 0.09 x 9.21 inches
Language: eng

Biennial report of the Board of State Harbor Commissioners, for the two fiscal years commencing July 1, 1890, and ending June 30, 1892

Various

www.triestepublishing.com

You May Also Like

ISBN: 9780649199693
Paperback: 48 pages
Dimensions: 6.14 x 0.10 x 9.21 inches
Language: eng

Biennial report of the Board of State Harbor Commissioners for the two fisca years. Commeneing July 1, 1884, and Ending June 30, 1886

Various

ISBN: 9780649196395
Paperback: 44 pages
Dimensions: 6.14 x 0.09 x 9.21 inches
Language: eng

Biennial report of the Board of state commissioners, for the two fiscal years, commencing July 1, 1890, and ending June 30, 1892

Various

Find more of our titles on our website. We have a selection of thousands of titles that will interest you. Please visit

www.triestepublishing.com

Lightning Source UK Ltd.
Milton Keynes UK
UKOW01f1323231017
311488UK00017B/3804/P

9 780649 587278